1st World Library

Literary Society

Classic Series

Book Catalog

1st World Library – Literary Society

1100 North 4th Street
Fairfield, Iowa 52556
877-209-5004
cataloginfo@1stworldlibrary.ORG

www.1stworldlibrary.ORG

CATALOG AND RETAIL PRICE LIST
OCTOBER 1, 2005

1st World Library – Literary Society is a nonprofit organization dedicated to promoting literary by:

Creating a free internet library accessible from any computer worldwide.

Hosting writing competitions and offering book publishing scholarships.

Copyright - 1st World Library – Literary Society, 2003, 2004, 2005

ORDERING INFORMATION

1) We are constantly adding new titles to our catalog. The most current catalog can be viewed and printed online at www.1stWorldLibrary.org/catalog/

2) All titles in our catalog can be ordered directly from our retail site online at www.1stWorldLibrary.ORG, this online site accepts Master Card and Visa.

3) To send in an order by mail please fill out a Book Order form and send it with your payment to the address on the form. These forms can be printed from our site at www.1stWorldLibrary.org/orderform/

4) Discount pricing is available for bookstores, schools and libraries. Please call 877-209-5004 to register and qualify for discount pricing.

5) Inquiries may be sent to:

                1st World Library – Literary Society
                1100 North 4th Street
                Fairfield, Iowa 52556
                877-209-5004
                cataloginfo@1stworldlibrary.org

WRITING COMPETITIONS AND BOOK SCHOLARSHIPS

1st World Library Literary Society is proud to sponsor Poetry Writing Competitions designed to promote creative writing and literacy skills in grades 1 through 12. These writing competitions provide a unique opportunity for students to learn how to write poetry and to have the experience of being published. The local organizers or school teachers will set the themes and rules of the competitions and will also select the top poems to be submitted to 1st World Library for inclusion a standard 6 x 9 perfect bound soft cover book. Introductions to the poetry book can be written by the Principal of the school, the Mayor, or other local business and community leaders.

1st World Library Literary Society will provide a full book publishing scholarship. The scholarship covers the cost of creating a full color book cover, text formatting, obtaining an ISBN, Library of Congress Catalogue numbers and publishing the book through standard publishing channels. The finished book will be available online through Amazon, Barnes & Noble, etc. and through bookstores worldwide.

A portion of all book sales are donated to the school or library and the sale of the poetry book can be used for fundraising. Many schools have set up their own book signings at local libraries and schools. At these book signings, the children have the opportunity to read their poems to family and friends, and the general public invited to celebrate their creativity.

To schedule a poetry writing competition for your school or library call 1st World Library at 877-209-5004 or visit us online at www.1stworldlibrary.org

FREE INTERNET LIBRARY

Welcome to 1ˢᵗ World Library's *free* classic e-book library. Our mission is to make the world's best classic literature available to everyone as an instrument for higher education and achievement. It doesn't matter whether you are working at home, in the office, or even on vacation, if you have access to a computer and the Internet you can access our free Internet library of classic books.

Anyone can become a member of 1ˢᵗ World Library by registering online. Once you become a member you will have access to our complete online library of classic downloadable e-books at no charge. All of the titles listed in this catalog are available in downloadable e-book format. Each month, new titles are being digitized and will be made available online for download from our web site: www.1stworldlibrary.org.

EBOOKS ON CD

To begin your collection of classic e-books you can order our EBOOKS ON CD, which contains 200 classic e-books in easy-to-view PDF format. These e-books can be viewed from the CD or loaded on to your computer or network for viewing. The EBOOKS ON CD is free for schools and libraries; all others are charged a small fee of $25 to offset production costs.

To order your EBOOKS ON CD,
call 877-209-5004

TABLE OF CONTENTS

Titles Listed Alphabetically 18

Titles Listed by Author Name 50

    Aaronsohn, Alexander 50
    Abbot, Jacob 50
    Abbot, L. A. 50
    Abhedananda, Swami 50
    Abrahams, Israel 50
    Ackland, T. S. 50
    Adams, Andy 50
    Adams, Henry 50
    Adams, M. H. 50
    Adams, Samuel Hopkins 50
    Ade, George 50
    Aesop 50
    Alcott, Louisa May 50
    Aldrich, Thomas Bailey 51
    Alger, Horatio 51
    Alger Jr., Horatio 51
    Allen, Grant 51
    Allen, James 52
    Allen, James Lane 52
    Allison, Samuel B. 52
    Allison, Young E. 52
    Altsheler, Joseph A. 52
    Alvares, Rahul 52
    Andersen, Hans Christian 52
    Anderson, Robert Gordon 52
    Anderson, Sherwood 52
    Anderton, Thomas 52

Andrews, James 52
Andreyev, Leonid 52
Angellotti, Marion Polk 52
Anonymous 52
Appleton, Victor 52
Arnold, Edwin L. 53
Arthur, T. S. 53
Atherton, Gertrude 53
Atkins, Eleanor 53
Atticus 53
Austen, Jane 53
Austin, J. G. 54
Austin, Mary 54
Avery, Harold 54
Azuela, Mariano 54
Bacheller, Irving 54
Bacon, Francis 54
Baden-Powell, B.H. 54
Badger Jr, Joseph E. 54
Bagnold, Enid 54
Bailey, H.C. 54
Baker, Willard F. 54
Baldwin, James 54
Ball, R. S. 54
Ballantyne, Robert Michael 54
Bangs, John Kendrick 54
Barbour, Ralph Henry 54
Barbusse, Henri 54
Barr, Amelia E. 54
Barr, Robert 54
Barrie, J. M. 54
Baum, L. Frank 55
Beach, Rex 55
Beach, Rex E. 55
Beerbohm, Max 55
Beethoven, Ludwig van 55
Bell, John Joy 55
Bell, Lilian 55
Bennett, Arnold 55
Benson, Stella 55

Bernhardt, Sarah 55
Besant, Annie 55
Bierce, Ambrose 55
Bjornson, Bjornstjerne..55
Bosher, Kate Langley 55
Bower, B. M. 55
Bower, Bertha Muzzy 55
Bradley, Mary Hastings 56
Braeme, Charlotte M. 56
Brebner, Percy 56
Browne, Charles Farrar...56
Bulfinch, Thomas..56
Burgess, Thornton W. 56
Burleigh, Cyril...56
Burnett, Frances Hodgson 56
Burroughs, Edgar Rice..56
Burroughs, John 57
Cable, Boyd...57
Cable, George W. 57
Call, Annie Payson 57
Camp, Walter..57
Carey, Joseph 57
Carey, Rosa Nouchette..57
Carroll, Lewis 57
Casson, Herbert N. 57
Cather, Willa...57
Chambers, Robert W. 57
Chekhov, Anton 57
Cheley, F. H...58
Chesterton, G. K. 58
Christie, Agatha..58
Churchill, Winston 58
Clark, Dougan 59
Clouston, J. Storer...59
Cody, H. A. 59
Cole, Mary 59
Collins, Wilkie 59
Collodi, C. 59
Confucius..59
Conrad, Joseph..59

Conscience, Hendrik 59
Corvus, M. 59
Cotes, Everard 59
Crane, Stephen 59
Cross, F. J. 59
Crowley, Mary Catherine 59
Curtis, Alice Turner 59
Curwood, James Oliver 59
Darlington, Edgar B. P. 59
Darwin, Francis 60
Daviess, Maria Thompson 60
Davis, Andrew McFarland 60
Davis, H. W. C. 60
Davis, R. H. 60
Davis, Richard Harding 60
Day Jr., Clarence 60
Balzac, Honore De 60
De Mille, James 60
Defoe, Daniel 60
Der Ling, The Princess 60
Descartes, Rene 60
Dickens, Charles 60
Dickinson, Emily 60
Donnell, Annie Hamilton 61
Dostoyevsky, Fyodor 61
Doyle, Arthur Conan 61
Drake, Robert L. 61
Driscoll, James R. 62
Dumas, Alexandre 62
Dunbar, Alice 62
Durston, George 62
Eastman, Charles A. 62
Ebers, George 62
Edgeworth, Maria 62
Ellis, Edward S. 62
Eliot, George 62
Emerson, Ralph Waldo 62
Everett-green, Evelyn 62
Fabre, J. Henri 62
Fairbanks, Douglas 62

Flaubert, Gustave	62
Fletcher, J. S.	63
Foa, Eugenie	63
Ford, Henry Jones	63
Freud, Sigmund	63
Frost, Henry	63
Frost, Robert	63
Gallienne, Richard Le	63
Garis, Howard R.	63
Garnett, David	63
Gaskell, Elizabeth	63
Gaskell, Elizabeth Cleghorn	63
Gatty, Mrs. Alfred	63
Gay, John	63
Giles, Herbert A.	63
Gillmore, Inez Haynes	63
Gilman, Charlotte Perkins Stetson	63
Glasworthy, John	63
Grahame, Kenneth	63
Grant, U. S.	63
Gregory, Eliot	64
Grey, Zane	64
Griswold, Latta	65
Habberton, John	65
Haggard, H. Rider	65
Hancock, H. Irving	65
Hardy, Thomas	65
Harris, Frank	65
Hawthorne, Nathaniel	65
Hawthrone, Julian	65
Hayes, Clair W.	65
Henty, G.A.	65
Hergesheimer, Joseph	65
Hesse, Herman	65
Hill, Frederick Trevor	65
Holmes, R. Derby	65
Homer	65
Hope, Laura Lee	66
Houdini, Harry	66
Hough, Emerson	66

Housman, Clemence 66
Housman, Laurence 66
Howells, William Dean 66
Huxley, Thomas H. 66
Ibsen, Henrik 66
Lie Jonas, Lauritz Idemil 67
Ingleby, C. M. 67
Irving, H. B. 67
Irving, Washington 67
Isham, Frederic Stewart 67
Ives, Charles 67
Jackson, Gabrielle E. 67
Jackson, Helent Hunt 67
Jacobs, Joseph 67
Jacobsen, Jens Peter 67
James, George Wharton 67
James, Henry 67
Janes, Don Carlos 67
Janvier, Thomas A. 67
Jefferies, Richard 67
Jerome, Jerome K. 67
Johnson, Owen 67
Jones, Erasmus W. 67
Joyce, James 67
Kay, Ross 67
Kelly, Myra 67
Kempis, Thomas A. 67
Kennedy, John F. 68
Kerst, Friedrich 68
Key, Ellen 68
Keyes, Frances Parkinson 68
Keyhole, Donald 68
Kielland, Alexander 68
Kilner, Dorothy 68
King, Basil 68
King, Grace E. 68
Kingsley, Charles 68
Kipling, Rudyard 68
Klein, Charles 68
Knowles, James Sheridan 68

Kyne, Peter B. 68
Lagerlof, Selma 68
Lang, Andrew 68
Lansing, Robert 68
Lawrence, D. H. 68
Lawton, Wilbur 68
Le Queux, William 68
Leroux, Gaston 68
Leverson, Ada 69
Lindsay, Maud 69
Lofting, Hugh 69
London, Jack 69
Longfellow, Henry Wadsworth 69
Lynd, Robert 69
Mabie, Hamilton Wright 69
Macartney Lane, Enilor 69
MacDonald, George 69
Machiavelli, Nicolo 69
Maclaren, Ian 69
Macomber, Ben 69
Macomber, C. E. 69
Mather, Frank Jewett 69
McCarthy, Justin Huntly 70
McCracken, Elizabeth 70
McGaffey, Kenneth 70
McGrath, Harold 70
Meade, L. T. 70
Meredith, George 70
Merriman, Henry Seton 70
Middleton, Lydia Miller 70
Miller, Alice Duer 70
Milton, John 70
Montgomery, Lucy Maud 70
More, Thomas 70
Mulford, Clarence E. 70
Mumford, Ethel Watts 70
Munro, H. H. 71
Nesbit, E. 71
Nicolay, Helen 71
Nietzsche, Friedrich 71

O'Biren, Edward J. ... 71
Ogg, Federick Austin ... 71
O'Grady, Standish ... 71
Okakura, Kakuzo ... 71
Ollivant, Alfred ... 71
Oppenheim, E. Phillips ... 71
Oppenheim, James ... 71
Orczy, Baroness ... 71
Orr, Lyndon ... 72
Orwell, George ... 72
Osbourne, Lloyd ... 72
Ossendowski, Ferdinand ... 72
Otis, James ... 72
Overton, Mark ... 72
Oxley, J. Macdonald ... 72
Ozaki, Yei Theodora ... 72
Pack, Charles Lathrop ... 72
Packard, Frank L. ... 72
Parmananda, Swami ... 72
Patchin, Frank Gee ... 72
Penrose, Margret ... 72
Perkins, Lucy Fitch ... 72
Plato ... 73
Poe, Edgar Allan ... 73
Pyle, Ernie Howard ... 73
Pyle, Howard ... 73
Queux, William Le ... 73
Quincey, Thomas De ... 73
Ramachakra, Yogi ... 73
Ransome, Arthur ... 73
Rhinehart, Mary Roberts ... 73
Roe, E. P. ... 73
Rowlandson, Mary ... 73
Sangster, Margaret E. ... 73
Scott, Walter ... 73
Serviss, Garrett P. ... 73
Seton-Thompson, Grace Gallatin ... 73
Severing, Paul ... 73
Sewell, Anna ... 73
Shaw, George Bernard ... 73

Shelley, Mary Wollstonecraft 75
Sherwell, Guillermo A. 75
Sousa, John Philip 75
Stevenson, R. L. 75
Stoker, Bram 76
Stokes, Katherine 76
Stowe, Harriet Beecher 76
Streuvels, Stijn 76
Swift, Jonathan 76
Tagore, Rabindranath 76
Tarkington, Booth 76
Taylor, Bayard 76
Taylor, Frederick Winslow 76
Thackeray, William Makepeace 76
Thoreau, Henry David 76
Thorne, Paul and Mabel 76
Thurston, Katherine Cecil 76
Tolstoy, Leo 76
Tomlinson, Paul G. 77
Tracy, Louis 77
Traill, Catherine Parr 77
Tucker, George 77
Turgenev, Ivan 77
Turner, Ethel 77
Twain, Mark 77
Van Dyne, Edith 78
Vandercook, Margaret 78
Various Authors 78
Verne, Jules 78
Von Arnim, Elizabeth 78
Walpole, Horace 78
Walpole, Hugh 78
Walter, William W. 78
Walton, O. F. 78
Ward, Adolphus William 79
Ward, Humphry 79
Warner, Charles Dudley 79
Webster, Frank V. 79
Wells, Carolyn 79
Wells, H. G. 79

Weyman, Stanley 79
Wharton, Edith 79
Whibley, Charles 79
White, Stewart Edward 79
Wilde, Oscar 79
Willcox, Cornelis DeWitt 80
Williams, Valentine 80
Willing, Charles 80
Winfield, Arthur M. 80
Wodehouse, P. G. 80
Wood, Eugene 80
Woolf, Virginia 80
Yonge, Charlotte M 81
Zollinger, Gulielma 81

TITLES LISTED ALPHABETICALLY

ISBN	TITLE	AUTHOR	RETAIL	EDITION
1-59540-027-3	A Book of Remarkable Criminals	Irving, H. B.	$14.95	Softcover
1-59540-012-5	A Book of Scoundrels	Whibley, Charles	$12.95	Softcover
1-4218-0449-2	A Boy's Ride	Zollinger, Gulielma	$13.95	Softcover
1-59540-117-2	A Boy's Will	Frost, Robert	$10.95	Softcover
1-59540-549-6	A Changed Man	Hardy, Thomas	$15.95	Softcover
1-59540-010-9	A Christmas Carol	Dickens, Charles	$10.95	Softcover
1-4218-0610-X	A Christmas Carol	Dickens, Charles	$26.95	Hardcover
1-59540-310-8	A Connecticut Yankee In King Arthur's Court	Twain, Mark	$17.95	Softcover
1-59540-339-6	A Damsel In Distress	Wodehouse, P. G.	$14.95	Softcover
1-4218-1570-2	A Daughter of the Snows	London, Jack	$15.95	Softcover
1-4218-1534-6	A Double Story	Macdonald, George	$10.95	Softcover
1-59540-500-3	A Familiar Study Of Men And Books	Stevenson, R. L.	$14.95	Softcover
1-59540-128-8	A Far Country, Vol1	Churchill, Winston	$12.95	Softcover
1-59540-129-6	A Far Country, Vol2	Churchill, Winston	$12.95	Softcover
1-4218-1583-4	A Garland for Girls	Alcott, Louisa May	$12.95	Softcover
1-4218-0166-3	A Girl of the People	Meade, L. T.	$12.95	Softcover
1-4218-0456-5	A Great Success	Ward, Humphry	$10.95	Softcover
1-59540-518-6	A Group Of Noble Dames	Hardy, Thomas	$13.95	Softcover
1-4218-1516-8	A Happy Boy	Bjornson, Bjornstjerne	$10.95	Softcover
1-4218-0436-0	A Heroine of France	Everett-Green, Evelyn	$13.95	Softcover
1-59540-311-6	A Horse's Tale	Twain, Mark	$10.95	Softcover
1-4218-0403-4	A Knight of the Nets	Barr, Amelia E.	$13.95	Softcover
1-4218-1137-5	A Man and His Money	Isham, Frederic Stewart	$13.95	Softcover
1-59540-519-4	A Pair Of Blue Eyes	Hardy, Thomas	$21.95	Softcover
1-4218-0869-2	A Pair Of Blue Eyes	Hardy, Thomas	$39.95	Hardcover

ISBN	TITLE	AUTHOR	RETAIL	EDITION
1-4218-0475-1	A Peep Behind the Scenes	Walton, O. F.	$13.95	Softcover
1-4218-0443-3	A Question	Ebers, Georg	$10.95	Softcover
1-4218-1153-7	A Rebellious Heroine	Bangs, John Kendrick	$10.95	Softcover
1-59540-025-7	A Simple Soul	Flaubert, Gustave	$10.95	Softcover
1-59540-400-7	A Study In Scarlet	Doyle, Arthur Conan	$11.95	Softcover
1-4218-0167-1	A Sweet Girl Graduate	Meade, L. T.	$14.95	Softcover
1-4218-0197-3	A Tale of One City	Anderton, Thomas	$10.95	Softcover
1-59540-419-8	A Tale Of Two Cities	Dickens, Charles	$21.95	Softcover
1-4218-0819-6	A Tale Of Two Cities	Dickens, Charles	$39.95	Hardcover
1-4218-1105-7	A Texas Matchmaker	Adams, Andy	$13.95	Softcover
1-59540-130-X	A Traveller In War Time	Churchill, Winston	$10.95	Softcover
1-59540-235-7	A Treatise on Parents and Children	Shaw, George Bernard	$11.95	Softcover
1-4218-0735-1	A Treatise on Parents and Children	Shaw, George Bernard	$26.95	Hardcover
1-4218-0428-X	A Trip Abroad	Janes, Don Carlos	$11.95	Softcover
1-4218-0444-1	A Voyage to the Moon	Tucker, George	$13.95	Softcover
1-4218-0447-6	A Woman Tenderfoot	Seton-Thompson, Grace Gallatin	$10.95	Softcover
1-4218-0401-8	A Yankee Girl at Fort Sumter	Curtis, Alice Turner	$11.95	Softcover
1-4218-0480-8	A Yankee in the Trenches	Holmes, R. Derby	$11.95	Softcover
1-59540-691-3	A Young Girl's Diary	Freud, Sigmund	$13.95	Softcover
1-59540-618-2	Aaron's Rod	Lawrence, D. H.	$20.95	Softcover
1-59540-013-3	Abbeychurch	Yonge, Charlotte M	$14.95	Softcover
1-59540-502-X	Across The Plains	Stevenson, R. L.	$12.95	Softcover
1-4218-0852-8	Across The Plains	Stevenson, R. L.	$27.95	Hardcover
1-4218-1116-2	Action Front	Cable, Boyd	$12.95	Softcover
1-59540-600-X	Aesop's Fables	Aesop	$11.95	Softcover
1-4218-0193-0	After A Shadow	Arthur, T. S.	$11.95	Softcover
1-4218-0194-9	After The Storm	Arthur, T. S.	$13.95	Softcover
1-59540-444-9	Alcibiades I & II	Plato	$11.95	Softcover
1-59540-698-0	Alexander's Bridge	Cather, Willa	$10.95	Softcover
1-4218-1115-4	Alice Adams	Tarkington, Booth	$14.95	Softcover
1-59540-442-2	Alice's Adventure In Wonderland	Carroll, Lewis	$10.95	Softcover
1-4218-0842-0	Alice's Adventure In Wonderland	Carroll, Lewis	$26.95	Hardcover
1-59540-312-4	Alonzo Fitz And Other Stories	Twain, Mark	$10.95	Softcover
1-59540-672-7	American Fairy Tales	Baum, L. Frank	$10.95	Softcover

ISBN	TITLE	AUTHOR	RETAIL	EDITION
1-59540-634-4	An African Millionaire	Allen, Grant	$13.95	Softcover
1-4218-0186-8	An American Robinson Crusoe	Allison, Samuel B.	$10.95	Softcover
1-4218-0114-0	An Amiable Charlatan	Oppenheim, E. Phillips	$13.95	Softcover
1-59540-644-1	An Enemy of the People	Ibsen, Henrik	$11.95	Softcover
1-4218-0944-3	An Enemy of the People	Ibsen, Henrik	$26.95	Hardcover
1-59540-332-9	An Ideal Husband	Wilde, Oscar	$11.95	Softcover
1-4218-0782-3	An Ideal Husband	Wilde, Oscar	$26.95	Hardcover
1-59540-501-1	An InLand Voyage	Stevenson, R. L.	$10.95	Softcover
1-4218-0851-X	An InLand Voyage	Stevenson, R. L.	$26.95	Hardcover
1-59540-200-4	An Introduction To Yoga	Besant, Annie	$10.95	Softcover
1-4218-1584-2	An Old Fashioned Girl	Alcott, Louisa May	$14.95	Softcover
1-4218-1548-6	An Old Maid	De Balzac, Honore	$11.95	Softcover
1-4218-0198-1	An Old Town By The Sea	Aldrich, Thomas Bailey	$10.95	Softcover
1-59540-236-5	An Unsocial Socialist	Shaw, George Bernard	$15.95	Softcover
1-59540-305-1	Andersen's Fairy Tales	Andersen, Hans Christian	$12.95	Softcover
1-4218-0755-6	Andersen's Fairy Tales	Andersen, Hans Christian	$27.95	Hardcover
1-59540-237-3	Androcles and The Lion	Shaw, George Bernard	$10.95	Softcover
1-4218-1146-4	Angel Island	Gillmore, Inez Haynes	$12.95	Softcover
1-59540-429-5	Animal Farm	Orwell, George	$10.95	Softcover
1-4218-0829-3	Animal Farm	Orwell, George	$26.95	Hardcover
1-59540-109-1	Anne Of Avonlea	Montgomery, Lucy Maud	$15.95	Softcover
1-4218-0659-2	Anne Of Avonlea	Montgomery, Lucy Maud	$31.95	Hardcover
1-59540-110-5	Anne Of Green Gables	Montgomery, Lucy Maud	$17.95	Softcover
1-4218-0660-6	Anne Of Green Gables	Montgomery, Lucy Maud	$33.95	Hardcover
1-4218-1172-3	Apples, Ripe and Rosy, Sir,	Crowley, Mary Catherine	$11.95	Softcover
1-4218-0492-1	Arizona Nights	White, Stewart Edward	$13.95	Softcover
1-59540-238-1	Arms and the Man	Shaw, George Bernard	$10.95	Softcover
1-4218-0738-6	Arms and the Man	Shaw, George Bernard	$26.95	Hardcover
1-59540-042-7	Around the World in 80 Days	Verne, Jules	$13.95	Softcover
1-4218-0642-8	Around the World in 80 Days	Verne, Jules	$28.95	Hardcover
1-59540-208-X	At The Earths Core	Burroughs, Edgar Rice	$11.95	Softcover

ISBN	TITLE	AUTHOR	RETAIL	EDITION
1-4218-0708-4	At The Earths Core	Burroughs, Edgar Rice	$26.95	Hardcover
1-4218-1125-1	Aunt Jane's Nieces	Van Dyne, Edith	$12.95	Softcover
1-4218-1124-3	Aunt Jane's Nieces and Uncle John	Van Dyne, Edith	$11.95	Softcover
1-4218-1126-X	Aunt Jane's Nieces at Millville	Van Dyne, Edith	$12.95	Softcover
1-4218-1523-0	Aunt Jane's Nieces at Work	Van Dyne, Edith	$12.95	Softcover
1-4218-1524-9	Aunt Jane's Nieces in Society	Van Dyne, Edith	$13.95	Softcover
1-4218-1127-8	Aunt Jane's Nieces on Vacation	Van Dyne, Edith	$12.95	Softcover
1-4218-1525-7	Aunt Jane's Nieces out West	Van Dyne, Edith	$12.95	Softcover
1-59540-681-6	Aunt Judy's Tales	Gatty, Mrs. Alfred	$11.95	Softcover
1-4218-1185-5	Average Jones	Adams, Samuel Hopkins	$13.95	Softcover
1-59540-629-8	Back Home	Wood, Eugene	$12.95	Softcover
1-59540-660-3	Back to God's Country	Curwood, James Oliver	$13.95	Softcover
1-4218-0960-5	Back to God's Country	Curwood, James Oliver	$28.95	Hardcover
1-4218-0446-8	Balcony Stories	King, Grace E.	$10.95	Softcover
1-59540-617-4	Bar-20 Days	Mulford, Clarence E.	$13.95	Softcover
1-59540-661-1	Baree, Son of Kazan	Curwood, James Oliver	$12.95	Softcover
1-4218-0961-3	Baree, Son of Kazan	Curwood, James Oliver	$27.95	Hardcover
1-4218-0407-7	Beasley's Christmas Party	Tarkington, Booth	$10.95	Softcover
1-59540-638-7	Beasts and Super-Beasts	Munro, H. H.	$13.95	Softcover
1-4218-0126-4	Beasts, Men and Gods	Ossendowski, Ferdinand	$14.95	Softcover
1-4218-0026-8	Beasts, Men and Gods	Ossendowski, Ferdinand	$29.95	Hardcover
1-59540-625-5	Beautiful Stories from Shakespeare	Nesbit, E.	$12.95	Softcover
1-4218-0925-7	Beautiful Stories from Shakespeare	Nesbit, E.	$27.95	Hardcover
1-59540-006-0	Beauty and The Beast	Taylor, Bayard	$14.95	Softcover
1-4218-0606-1	Beauty and The Beast	Taylor, Bayard	$29.95	Hardcover
1-59540-149-0	Beethoven: The Man and the Artist	Beethoven, Ludwig van	$10.95	Softcover
1-4218-0699-1	Beethoven: The Man and the Artist	Beethoven, Ludwig van	$26.95	Hardcover
1-4218-0458-1	Before Adam	London, Jack	$10.95	Softcover
1-4218-0358-5	Before Adam	London, Jack	$26.95	Hardcover
1-4218-0414-X	Being A Boy	Warner, Charles Dudley	$10.95	Softcover

ISBN	TITLE	AUTHOR	RETAIL	EDITION
1-59540-631-X	Beneath The Banner	Cross, F. J.	$12.95	Softcover
1-4218-0149-3	Beside The Bonnie Brier Bush	Maclaren, Ian	$12.95	Softcover
1-59540-532-1	Betty Zane	Grey, Zane	$15.95	Softcover
1-59540-643-3	Between Whiles	Jackson, Helent Hunt	$12.95	Softcover
1-59540-022-2	Beyond Good and Evil	Nietzsche, Friedrich	$12.95	Softcover
1-4218-0622-3	Beyond Good and Evil	Nietzsche, Friedrich	$27.95	Hardcover
1-59540-401-5	Beyond The City	Doyle, Arthur Conan	$11.95	Softcover
1-59540-112-1	Biographical Stories	Hawthorne, Nathaniel	$10.95	Softcover
1-59540-041-9	Birds and Poets	Burroughs, John	$12.95	Softcover
1-59540-605-0	Black Beauty	Sewell, Anna	$12.95	Softcover
1-59540-639-5	Black Heart and White Heart	Haggard, H. Rider	$10.95	Softcover
1-4218-0478-6	Bob Cook and the German Spy	Tomlinson, Paul G.	$12.95	Softcover
1-4218-0141-8	Bound To Rise	Alger Jr., Horatio	$13.95	Softcover
1-4218-0041-1	Bound To Rise	Alger Jr., Horatio	$28.95	Hardcover
1-4218-1552-4	Brave and Bold	Alger Jr., Horatio	$13.95	Softcover
1-4218-1134-0	Buffalo Roost	Cheley, F.H.	$12.95	Softcover
1-4218-0429-8	Bunner Sisters	Wharton, Edith	$10.95	Softcover
1-4218-1165-0	Bunny Brown and his Sister Sue	Hope, Laura Lee	$11.95	Softcover
1-59540-430-9	Burmese Days	Orwell, George	$15.95	Softcover
1-4218-0830-7	Burmese Days	Orwell, George	$31.95	Hardcover
1-4218-0462-X	By The Golden Gate	Carey, Joseph	$11.95	Softcover
1-4218-1111-1	Cabin Fever	Bower, B. M.	$11.95	Softcover
1-59540-239-X	Caesar And Cleopatra	Shaw, George Bernard	$11.95	Softcover
1-4218-0739-4	Caesar And Cleopatra	Shaw, George Bernard	$26.95	Hardcover
1-59540-240-3	Candida	Shaw, George Bernard	$10.95	Softcover
1-4218-0740-8	Candida	Shaw, George Bernard	$26.95	Hardcover
1-59540-241-1	Captain Brassbound's Conversion	Shaw, George Bernard	$10.95	Softcover
1-4218-0741-6	Captain Brassbound's Conversion	Shaw, George Bernard	$26.95	Hardcover
1-4218-1178-2	Captain Macklin	Davis, Richard Harding	$12.95	Softcover
1-59540-516-X	Captains Courageous	Kipling, Rudyard	$12.95	Softcover
1-4218-0473-5	Captivity and Restoration	Rowlandson, Mary	$10.95	Softcover
1-4218-1514-1	Casey Ryan	Bower, B. M.	$12.95	Softcover

ISBN	TITLE	AUTHOR	RETAIL	EDITION
1-4218-0471-9	Castle Rackrent	Edgeworth, Maria	$11.95	Softcover
1-4218-1198-7	Catherine: A Story	Thackeray, William Makepeace	$12.95	Softcover
1-59540-503-8	Catriona	Stevenson, R. L.	$15.95	Softcover
1-4218-0853-6	Catriona	Stevenson, R. L.	$31.95	Hardcover
1-59540-001-X	Chaucer	Ward, Adolphus William	$12.95	Softcover
1-4218-0601-0	Chaucer	Ward, Adolphus William	$27.95	Hardcover
1-59540-313-2	Christian Science	Twain, Mark	$13.95	Softcover
1-59540-000-1	Cinderella	Anonymous	$10.95	Softcover
1-4218-0600-2	Cinderella	Anonymous	$26.95	Hardcover
1-4218-0459-X	Cleopatra	Abbott, Jacob	$12.95	Softcover
1-59540-431-7	Coming Up For Air	Orwell, George	$13.95	Softcover
1-4218-0831-5	Coming Up For Air	Orwell, George	$28.95	Hardcover
1-4218-0416-6	Coralie	Braeme, Charlotte M.	$10.95	Softcover
1-4218-0421-2	Countess Kate	Yonge, Charlotte M.	$12.95	Softcover
1-59540-627-1	Cousin Phillis	Gaskell, Elizabeth Cleghorn	$10.95	Softcover
1-4218-0927-3	Cousin Phillis	Gaskell, Elizabeth Cleghorn	$26.95	Hardcover
1-4218-1112-X	Creation and Its Records	Badhen-Powell, B. H.	$12.95	Softcover
1-59540-685-9	Cuba In War Time	Davis, Richard Harding	$10.95	Softcover
1-4218-1561-3	Curly and Floppy Twistytail	Garis, Howard R.	$11.95	Softcover
1-4218-1562-1	Daddy takes us to the Garden	Garis, Howard R.	$10.95	Softcover
1-4218-0451-4	Democracy An American Novel	Adams, Henry	$13.95	Softcover
1-59540-533-X	Desert Gold	Grey, Zane	$17.95	Softcover
1-4218-0883-8	Desert Gold	Grey, Zane	$33.95	Hardcover
1-4218-1563-X	Dick Hamiltons Airship	Garis, Howard R.	$13.95	Softcover
1-59540-449-X	Discourse On The Method Of Rightly...	Descartes, Rene	$10.95	Softcover
1-59540-131-8	Dr. Jonathan	Churchill, Winston	$10.95	Softcover
1-4218-1553-2	Driven From Home	Alger Jr., Horatio	$14.95	Softcover
1-59540-437-6	Dubliners	Joyce, James	$13.95	Softcover
1-4218-0837-4	Dubliners	Joyce, James	$28.95	Hardcover
1-59540-676-X	Eight Cousins	Alcott, Louisa May	$14.95	Softcover
1-59540-438-4	Emma	Austen, Jane	$22.95	Softcover
1-59540-670-0	English Fairy Tales	Jacobs, Joseph	$13.95	Softcover
1-59540-333-7	Essays and Lectures	Wilde, Oscar	$11.95	Softcover

ISBN	TITLE	AUTHOR	RETAIL	EDITION
1-4218-0783-1	Essays and Lectures	Wilde, Oscar	$26.95	Hardcover
1-59540-421-X	Essays Before a Sonata	Ives, Charles	$10.95	Softcover
1-59540-233-0	Essays of Francis Bacon	Bacon, Francis	$12.95	Softcover
1-4218-0733-5	Essays of Francis Bacon	Bacon, Francis	$27.95	Hardcover
1-59540-445-7	Essays Series 1	Emerson, Ralph Waldo	$13.95	Softcover
1-4218-0845-5	Essays Series 1	Emerson, Ralph Waldo	$28.95	Hardcover
1-59540-446-5	Essays Series 2	Emerson, Ralph Waldo	$11.95	Softcover
1-4218-0846-3	Essays Series 2	Emerson, Ralph Waldo	$26.95	Hardcover
1-59540-689-1	Esther	Carey, Rosa Nouchette	$14.95	Softcover
1-59540-307-8	Evangeline	Longfellow, Henry Wadsworth	$10.95	Softcover
1-59540-122-9	Evolution And Ethics	Huxley, Thomas H.	$15.95	Softcover
1-4218-0142-6	Facing The World	Alger Jr., Horatio	$11.95	Softcover
1-4218-0173-6	Famous Affinities of History, Vol 1	Orr, Lyndon	$10.95	Softcover
1-4218-0174-4	Famous Affinities of History, Vol 2	Orr, Lyndon	$10.95	Softcover
1-4218-0175-2	Famous Affinities of History, Vol 3	Orr, Lyndon	$10.95	Softcover
1-4218-0176-0	Famous Affinities of History, Vol 4	Orr, Lyndon	$10.95	Softcover
1-59540-242-X	Fanny's First Play	Shaw, George Bernard	$10.95	Softcover
1-4218-0742-4	Fanny's First Play	Shaw, George Bernard	$26.95	Hardcover
1-59540-520-8	Far From The Madding Crowd	Hardy, Thomas	$20.95	Softcover
1-59540-107-5	Flower Fables	Alcott, Louisa May	$10.95	Softcover
1-4218-0657-6	Flower Fables	Alcott, Louisa May	$26.95	Hardcover
1-59540-606-9	Four Girls and A Compact	Donnell, Annie Hamilton	$10.95	Softcover
1-59540-111-3	Frankenstein	Shelley, Mary Wollstonecraft	$13.95	Softcover
1-4218-0661-4	Frankenstein	Shelley, Mary Wollstonecraft	$28.95	Hardcover
1-4218-0180-9	Free From School	Alvares, Rahul	$10.95	Softcover
1-4218-0422-0	Friarswood Post-Office	Yonge, Charlotte M.	$13.95	Softcover
1-4218-1596-6	From A Bench in our Square	Adams, Samuel Hopkins	$14.95	Softcover
1-4218-0169-8	From A Girls Point Of View	Bell, Lilian	$10.95	Softcover
1-4218-0139-6	From One Generation to Another	Merriman, Henry Seton	$13.95	Softcover

ISBN	TITLE	AUTHOR	RETAIL	EDITION
1-59540-043-5	From the Earth to the Moon and Round the Moon	Verne, Jules	$17.95	Softcover
1-4218-0643-6	From the Earth to the Moon and Round the Moon	Verne, Jules	$33.95	Hardcover
1-59540-209-8	Gods Of Mars	Burroughs, Edgar Rice	$14.95	Softcover
1-4218-0709-2	Gods Of Mars	Burroughs, Edgar Rice	$29.95	Hardcover
1-4218-1593-1	Great Astronomers	Ball, R. S.	$13.95	Softcover
1-59540-420-1	Great Expectations	Dickens, Charles	$26.95	Softcover
1-4218-0820-X	Great Expectations	Dickens, Charles	$45.95	Hardcover
1-4218-0123-X	Greyfriars Bobby	Atkins, Eleanor	$12.95	Softcover
1-4218-0023-3	Greyfriars Bobby	Atkins, Eleanor	$27.95	Hardcover
1-4218-0423-9	Grisly Grisell	Yonge, Charlotte M.	$13.95	Softcover
1-4218-0431-X	Gulliver of Mars	Arnold, Edwin L.	$13.95	Softcover
1-59540-441-4	Gulliver's Travels	Swift, Jonathan	$15.95	Softcover
1-4218-0182-5	Half Past Seven Stories	Anderson, Robert Gordon	$12.95	Softcover
1-4218-0496-4	Happy Jack	Burgess, Thornton W.	$10.95	Softcover
1-59540-243-8	Heartbreak House	Shaw, George Bernard	$12.95	Softcover
1-4218-0743-2	Heartbreak House	Shaw, George Bernard	$27.95	Hardcover
1-59540-667-0	Helen's Babies	Habberton, John	$11.95	Softcover
1-4218-0143-4	Helping Himself	Alger Jr., Horatio	$13.95	Softcover
1-4218-1118-9	Herland	Gilman, Charlotte Perkins Stetson	$12.95	Softcover
1-59540-641-7	Heroes Every Child Should Know	Mabie, Hamilton Wright	$15.95	Softcover
1-4218-1544-3	Hilda Wade	Allen, Grant	$13.95	Softcover
1-4218-0408-5	His Own People	Tarkington, Booth	$10.95	Softcover
1-4218-0152-3	History of King Charles The Second of England	Abbot, Jacob	$12.95	Softcover
1-59540-108-3	Hospital Sketches	Alcott, Louisa May	$10.95	Softcover
1-4218-0658-4	Hospital Sketches	Alcott, Louisa May	$26.95	Hardcover
1-4218-1157-X	How It Happened	Bosher, Kate Langley	$10.95	Softcover
1-4218-0112-4	How to Live a Holy Life	Macomber, C. E.	$11.95	Softcover
1-59540-423-6	Humorous Tales	Poe, Edgar Allan	$13.95	Softcover
1-4218-0823-4	Humorous Tales	Poe, Edgar Allan	$28.95	Hardcover
1-59540-308-6	Hyperion	Longfellow, Henry Wadsworth	$14.95	Softcover
1-4218-0758-0	Hyperion	Longfellow, Henry Wadsworth	$29.95	Hardcover
1-4218-0108-6	I Will Repay	Orczy, Baroness Emmuska	$13.95	Softcover

ISBN	TITLE	AUTHOR	RETAIL	EDITION
1-4218-0008-X	I Will Repay	Orczy, Baroness Emmuska	$28.95	Hardcover
1-4218-0163-9	If I Were King	McCarthy, Justin Huntly	$12.95	Softcover
1-59540-148-2	Iliad of Homer	Homer	$18.95	Softcover
1-4218-0698-3	Iliad of Homer	Homer	$35.95	Hardcover
1-59540-645-X	In the Cage	James, Henry	$10.95	Softcover
1-4218-0413-1	In The Forest	Traill, Catherine Parr	$11.95	Softcover
1-4218-0185-X	In the Quarter	Chambers, Robert W.	$13.95	Softcover
1-4218-0196-5	In The Sargasso Sea	Janvier, Thomas A.	$13.95	Softcover
1-59540-504-6	In The South Seas	Stevenson, R. L.	$15.95	Softcover
1-4218-0854-4	In The South Seas	Stevenson, R. L.	$31.95	Hardcover
1-59540-604-2	Indian Games	Davis, Andrew McFarland	$10.95	Softcover
1-59540-009-5	Indian Heroes and Great Chieftains	Eastman, Charles A.	$10.95	Softcover
1-59540-340-X	Indiscretions of Archie	Wodehouse, P. G.	$15.95	Softcover
1-4218-0790-4	Indiscretions of Archie	Wodehouse, P. G.	$31.95	Hardcover
1-59540-334-5	Intentions	Wilde, Oscar	$12.95	Softcover
1-4218-0784-X	Intentions	Wilde, Oscar	$27.95	Hardcover
1-59540-201-2	Ivanoff	Chekhov, Anton	$10.95	Softcover
1-4218-1169-3	Jack and Jill	Alcott, Louisa May	$14.95	Softcover
1-4218-1138-3	Jack Archer	Henty, G.A.	$14.95	Softcover
1-4218-1136-7	Jack of the Pony Express	Webster, Frank V.	$11.95	Softcover
1-4218-0179-5	Jack Winters' Gridiron Chums	Overton, Mark	$11.95	Softcover
1-4218-1554-0	Jack's Ward	Alger Jr., Horatio	$13.95	Softcover
1-4218-0498-0	Jacob's Room	Woolf, Virginia	$12.95	Softcover
1-59540-147-4	Japanese Fairy Tales	Ozaki, Yei Theodora	$13.95	Softcover
1-4218-1156-1	Java Head	Hergesheimer, Joseph	$12.95	Softcover
1-4218-1151-0	Jerry of the Islands	London, Jack	$13.95	Softcover
1-4218-0144-2	Joe The Hotel Boy	Alger Jr., Horatio	$12.95	Softcover
1-4218-1555-9	Joe's Luck	Alger Jr., Horatio	$13.95	Softcover
1-59540-244-6	John Bull's Other Island	Shaw, George Bernard	$11.95	Softcover
1-4218-0744-0	John Bull's Other Island	Shaw, George Bernard	$26.95	Hardcover
1-4218-0150-7	Judaism	Abrahams, Israel	$10.95	Softcover
1-4218-1528-1	Katrine,	Macartney Lane, Enilor	$12.95	Softcover
1-4218-1194-4	Keeping Fit All the Way	Camp, Walter	$10.95	Softcover

ISBN	TITLE	AUTHOR	RETAIL	EDITION
1-59540-505-4	Kidnapped	Stevenson, R. L.	$14.95	Softcover
1-4218-0855-2	Kidnapped	Stevenson, R. L.	$29.95	Hardcover
1-4218-1585-0	Kitty's Class Day and Other Stories	Alcott, Louisa May	$13.95	Softcover
1-4218-0400-X	Ladies Must Live	Miller, Alice Duer	$11.95	Softcover
1-59540-621-2	Lady Into Fox	Garnett, David	$10.95	Softcover
1-4218-1518-4	Laugh and Live	Fairbanks, Douglas	$10.95	Softcover
1-59540-506-2	Lay Morals	Stevenson, R. L.	$14.95	Softcover
1-59540-805-3	Legends of Charlemagne	Bulfinch, Thomas	$17.95	Softcover
1-59540-314-0	Life On The Mississippi	Twain, Mark	$21.95	Softcover
1-59540-521-6	Lifes Little Ironies	Hardy, Thomas	$14.95	Softcover
1-59540-682-4	Little Citizens	Kelly, Myra	$11.95	Softcover
1-59540-335-3	Lord Arthur Savile's Crime	Wilde, Oscar	$11.95	Softcover
1-4218-0785-8	Lord Arthur Savile's Crime	Wilde, Oscar	$26.95	Hardcover
1-59540-040-0	Lost in the Fog	De Mille, James	$13.95	Softcover
1-59540-341-8	Love Among The Chickens	Wodehouse, P. G.	$12.95	Softcover
1-4218-0791-2	Love Among The Chickens	Wodehouse, P. G.	$27.95	Hardcover
1-4218-1102-2	Love at Second Sight	Leverson, Ada	$12.95	Softcover
1-4218-1591-5	Love Stories	Rhinehart, Mary Roberts	$13.95	Softcover
1-4218-0170-1	Love, The Fiddler	Osbourne, Lloyd	$11.95	Softcover
1-4218-1101-4	Love's Shadow	Leverson, Ada	$12.95	Softcover
1-4218-1564-8	Lulu, Alice and Jammie Wibble Wobble	Garis, Howard R.	$11.95	Softcover
1-59540-026-5	Madame Bovary	Flaubert, Gustave	$18.95	Softcover
1-4218-0626-6	Madame Bovary	Flaubert, Gustave	$35.95	Hardcover
1-59540-245-4	Major Barbara	Shaw, George Bernard	$11.95	Softcover
1-4218-0745-9	Major Barbara	Shaw, George Bernard	$26.95	Hardcover
1-4218-1556-7	Making His Way	Alger Jr., Horatio	$13.95	Softcover
1-59540-246-2	Man and Superman	Shaw, George Bernard	$13.95	Softcover
1-4218-0746-7	Man and Superman	Shaw, George Bernard	$28.95	Hardcover
1-59540-037-0	Mansfield Park	Austen, Jane	$21.95	Softcover
1-4218-0637-1	Mansfield Park	Austen, Jane	$39.95	Hardcover
1-4218-0488-3	Marching Men	Anderson, Sherwood	$13.95	Softcover
1-4218-0485-9	Martin Rattler	Ballantyne, Robert Michael	$12.95	Softcover
1-4218-0479-4	Marvels of Modern Science	Severing, Paul	$11.95	Softcover

ISBN	TITLE	AUTHOR	RETAIL	EDITION
1-4218-1549-4	Massimilla Doni	De Balzac, Honore	$10.95	Softcover
1-4218-0467-0	Master and Man	Tolstoy, Leo	$10.95	Softcover
1-59540-640-9	Medieval Europe	Davis, H. W. C.	$11.95	Softcover
1-59540-508-9	Memoir Of Fleeming Jenkin	Stevenson, R. L.	$11.95	Softcover
1-4218-0858-7	Memoir Of Fleeming Jenkin	Stevenson, R. L.	$26.95	Hardcover
1-59540-402-3	Memoirs Of Sherlock Holmes	Doyle, Arthur Conan	$14.95	Softcover
1-59540-507-0	Memories And Portraits	Stevenson, R. L.	$11.95	Softcover
1-4218-0857-9	Memories And Portraits	Stevenson, R. L.	$26.95	Hardcover
1-59540-017-6	Men Of Iron	Pyle, Ernie Howard	$13.95	Softcover
1-4218-0617-7	Men Of Iron	Pyle, Ernie Howard	$28.95	Hardcover
1-59540-692-1	Men, Women, and Boats	Crane, Stephen	$12.95	Softcover
1-4218-1545-1	Michael's Crag	Allen, Grant	$10.95	Softcover
1-59540-433-3	Miracle Mongers	Houdini, Harry	$11.95	Softcover
1-4218-0833-1	Miracle Mongers	Houdini, Harry	$26.95	Hardcover
1-59540-247-0	Misalliance	Shaw, George Bernard	$10.95	Softcover
1-4218-0747-5	Misalliance	Shaw, George Bernard	$26.95	Hardcover
1-59540-664-6	Mogens and Other Stories	Jacobsen, Jens Peter	$10.95	Softcover
1-4218-0964-8	Mogens and Other Stories	Jacobsen, Jens Peter	$26.95	Hardcover
1-59540-349-3	Monday or Tuesday	Woolf, Virginia	$10.95	Softcover
1-59540-659-X	Moon Face	London, Jack	$11.95	Softcover
1-4218-1592-3	Mother Stories	Lindsay, Maud	$10.95	Softcover
1-59540-234-9	Mozart The Man And The Artist	Kerst, Friedrich	$10.95	Softcover
1-59540-132-6	Mr. Crewes Career	Churchill, Winston	$24.95	Softcover
1-59540-248-9	Mrs Warren's Profession	Shaw, George Bernard	$10.95	Softcover
1-4218-0748-3	Mrs Warren's Profession	Shaw, George Bernard	$26.95	Hardcover
1-4218-0476-X	Murder in Any Degree	Johnson, Owen	$13.95	Softcover
1-4218-1130-8	My Lady Ludlow	Gaskell, Elizabeth	$12.95	Softcover
1-59540-034-6	My Life and Work	Ford, Henry Jones	$14.95	Softcover
1-4218-0634-7	My Life and Work	Ford, Henry Jones	$29.95	Hardcover
1-4218-1199-5	Mystic Christianity	Ramacharaka, Yogi	$12.95	Softcover
1-59540-509-7	New Arabian Nights	Stevenson, R. L.	$15.95	Softcover
1-4218-0859-5	New Arabian Nights	Stevenson, R. L.	$31.95	Hardcover
1-59540-530-5	Night And Day	Woolf, Virginia	$22.95	Softcover
1-59540-432-5	Nineteen Eighty Four	Orwell, George	$15.95	Softcover

ISBN	TITLE	AUTHOR	RETAIL	EDITION
1-4218-0832-3	Nineteen Eighty Four	Orwell, George	$31.95	Hardcover
1-59540-662-X	Nomads of The North	Curwood, James Oliver	$12.95	Softcover
1-4218-0962-1	Nomads of The North	Curwood, James Oliver	$27.95	Hardcover
1-59540-118-0	North of Boston	Frost, Robert	$10.95	Softcover
1-4218-0160-4	Northanger Abbey	Austen, Jane	$14.95	Softcover
1-59540-023-0	Notes from the Underground	Dostoyevsky, Fyodor	$11.95	Softcover
1-4218-0623-1	Notes from the Underground	Dostoyevsky, Fyodor	$26.95	Hardcover
1-59540-115-6	Notes of a War Correspondent	Davis, R. H.	$11.95	Softcover
1-4218-1180-4	October Vagabonds	Gallienne, Richard Le	$10.95	Softcover
1-4218-0155-8	Old Greek Stories	Baldwin, James	$11.95	Softcover
1-59540-426-0	Old World Romances	Poe, Edgar Allan	$10.95	Softcover
1-4218-0826-9	Old World Romances	Poe, Edgar Allan	$26.95	Hardcover
1-59540-133-4	On The American Contribution	Churchill, Winston	$10.95	Softcover
1-59540-021-4	On the Trail of Grant and Lee	Hill, Frederick Trevor	$12.95	Softcover
1-4218-0181-7	One Days Courtship and the Heralds of Fame	Barr, Robert	$11.95	Softcover
1-4218-1576-1	One of Life's Slaves	Idemil Lie, Jonas Lauritz	$11.95	Softcover
1-59540-020-6	Oscar Wilde, His Life and Confessions, Volume 1	Harris, Frank	$13.95	Softcover
1-4218-0620-7	Oscar Wilde, His Life and Confessions, Volume 1	Harris, Frank	$28.95	Hardcover
1-59540-610-7	Our Churches and Chapels	Atticus	$15.95	Softcover
1-4218-0434-4	Out of the Ashes	Mumford, Ethel Watts	$12.95	Softcover
1-59540-228-4	Out Of Times Abyss	Burroughs, Edgar Rice	$10.95	Softcover
1-59540-436-8	Outpost	Austin, J. G.	$14.95	Softcover
1-59540-048-6	Paradise Lost	Milton, John	$14.95	Softcover
1-4218-0648-7	Paradise Lost	Milton, John	$29.95	Hardcover
1-59540-049-4	Paradise Regained	Milton, John	$10.95	Softcover
1-4218-0482-4	Pardners	Beach, Rex E.	$11.95	Softcover
1-4218-0409-3	Patty's Butterfly Days	Wells, Carolyn	$13.95	Softcover
1-4218-0412-3	Patty's Suitors	Wells, Carolyn	$14.95	Softcover
1-59540-632-8	Peggy Stewart: Navy Girl at Home	Jackson, Gabrielle E.	$12.95	Softcover
1-59540-229-2	Pellucidar	Burroughs, Edgar Rice	$12.95	Softcover
1-59540-230-6	People Out Of Time	Burroughs, Edgar Rice	$10.95	Softcover
1-4218-0730-0	People Out Of Time	Burroughs, Edgar Rice	$26.95	Hardcover
1-59540-038-9	Persuasion	Austen, Jane	$14.95	Softcover

ISBN	TITLE	AUTHOR	RETAIL	EDITION
1-4218-0638-X	Persuasion	Austen, Jane	$29.95	Hardcover
1-4218-1517-6	Pictures from Italy	Dickens, Charles	$12.95	Softcover
1-4218-0417-4	Pigeon Pie	Yonge, Charlotte M.	$10.95	Softcover
1-59540-336-1	Poems	Wilde, Oscar	$13.95	Softcover
1-4218-0786-6	Poems	Wilde, Oscar	$28.95	Hardcover
1-59540-015-X	Poems, Series 1	Dickinson, Emily	$10.95	Softcover
1-59540-016-8	Poems, Series 2	Dickinson, Emily	$10.95	Softcover
1-4218-0616-9	Poems, Series 2	Dickinson, Emily	$26.95	Hardcover
1-4218-1597-2	Poor White	Anderson, Sherwood	$15.95	Softcover
1-4218-0402-6	Present at a Hanging	Bierce, Ambrose	$10.95	Softcover
1-59540-440-6	Pride and prejudice	Austen, Jane	$18.95	Softcover
1-4218-0840-4	Pride and prejudice	Austen, Jane	$35.95	Hardcover
1-59540-231-4	Princess Of Mars	Burroughs, Edgar Rice	$13.95	Softcover
1-59540-249-7	Pygmalion	Shaw, George Bernard	$11.95	Softcover
1-4218-0749-1	Pygmalion	Shaw, George Bernard	$26.95	Hardcover
1-4218-1196-0	Questionable Shapes	Howells, William Dean	$11.95	Softcover
1-4218-0445-X	Quit Your Worrying	James, George Wharton	$12.95	Softcover
1-4218-1557-5	Ragged Dick	Alger Jr., Horatio	$12.95	Softcover
1-4218-0410-7	Raspberry Jam	Wells, Carolyn	$13.95	Softcover
1-59540-686-7	Real Soldiers of Fortune	Davis, Richard Harding	$11.95	Softcover
1-59540-607-7	Rebecca Mary	Donnell, Annie Hamilton	$10.95	Softcover
1-4218-0135-3	Recalled To Life	Allen, Grant	$12.95	Softcover
1-59540-510-0	Records Of A Family Of Engineers	Stevenson, R. L.	$12.95	Softcover
1-59540-447-3	Representative Men	Emerson, Ralph Waldo	$12.95	Softcover
1-4218-0847-1	Representative Men	Emerson, Ralph Waldo	$27.95	Hardcover
1-59540-534-8	Riders Of Purple Sage	Grey, Zane	$17.95	Softcover
1-4218-1558-3	Risen From the Ranks	Alger Jr., Horatio	$13.95	Softcover
1-59540-619-0	Robinson Crusoe	Defoe, Daniel	$15.95	Softcover
1-4218-0919-2	Robinson Crusoe	Defoe, Daniel	$31.95	Hardcover
1-59540-403-1	Rodney Stone	Doyle, Arthur Conan	$14.95	Softcover
1-4218-1586-9	Rose in Bloom	Alcott, Louisa May	$14.95	Softcover
1-59540-315-9	Roughing It	Twain, Mark	$22.95	Softcover
1-4218-0765-3	Roughing It	Twain, Mark	$41.95	Hardcover

ISBN	TITLE	AUTHOR	RETAIL	EDITION
1-59540-404-X	Round The Red Lamp	Doyle, Arthur Conan	$13.95	Softcover
1-4218-0130-2	Salted With Fire	MacDonald, George	$13.95	Softcover
1-4218-1565-6	Sammie and Susie Littletail	Garis, Howard R.	$11.95	Softcover
1-59540-337-X	Selected Prose of Oscar Wilde	Wilde, Oscar	$11.95	Softcover
1-4218-0787-4	Selected Prose of Oscar Wilde	Wilde, Oscar	$26.95	Hardcover
1-59540-439-2	Sense and Sensibility	Austen, Jane	$17.95	Softcover
1-4218-0839-0	Sense and Sensibility	Austen, Jane	$33.95	Hardcover
1-4218-0433-6	Seven Little Australians	Turner, Ethel	$12.95	Softcover
1-4218-0183-3	Seven O'Clock Stories	Anderson, Robert Gordon	$11.95	Softcover
1-4218-0164-7	Seven Wives and Seven Prisons	Abbot, L. A.	$10.95	Softcover
1-59540-613-1	Shakespeare's Bones	Ingleby, C. M.	$10.95	Softcover
1-4218-0452-2	Siddhartha	Hesse, Herman	$11.95	Softcover
1-4218-0352-6	Siddhartha	Hesse, Herman	$26.95	Hardcover
1-59540-428-7	Silas Marner	Eliot, George	$13.95	Softcover
1-4218-0828-5	Silas Marner	Eliot, George	$28.95	Hardcover
1-4218-0448-4	Simon Bolivar	Sherwell, Guillermo A.	$12.95	Softcover
1-59540-206-3	Sir Nigel	Doyle, Arthur Conan	$18.95	Softcover
1-4218-0706-8	Sir Nigel	Doyle, Arthur Conan	$35.95	Hardcover
1-4218-1171-5	Sister Carmen	Corvus, M.	$10.95	Softcover
1-4218-1166-9	Six Little Bunkers at Grandma Bell's	Hope, Laura Lee	$11.95	Softcover
1-59540-316-7	Sketches New And Old	Twain, Mark	$17.95	Softcover
1-4218-0766-1	Sketches New And Old	Twain, Mark	$33.95	Hardcover
1-4218-0133-7	Sleeping Fires	Atherton, Gertrude	$12.95	Softcover
1-4218-0177-9	Small Means And Great Ends	Adams, M. H.	$10.95	Softcover
1-59540-309-4	State Of The Union Addresses	Kennedy, John F.	$10.95	Softcover
1-59540-527-5	Stories By English Authors In Africa	Various Authors	$11.95	Softcover
1-59540-528-3	Stories By English Authors In France	Various Authors	$11.95	Softcover
1-59540-529-1	Stories By English Authors In Germany	Various Authors	$11.95	Softcover
1-59540-633-6	Strong Hearts	Cable, George W.	$12.95	Softcover
1-59540-443-0	Sylvie And Bruno	Carroll, Lewis	$14.95	Softcover
1-4218-0843-9	Sylvie And Bruno	Carroll, Lewis	$29.95	Hardcover
1-59540-626-3	Taken Alive	Roe, E. P.	$17.95	Softcover
1-59540-424-4	Tales Of Illusion	Poe, Edgar Allan	$10.95	Softcover

ISBN	TITLE	AUTHOR	RETAIL	EDITION
1-4218-0824-2	Tales Of Illusion	Poe, Edgar Allan	$26.95	Hardcover
1-4218-0430-1	Tales of Men and Ghosts	Wharton, Edith	$15.95	Softcover
1-59540-425-2	Tales Of Science	Poe, Edgar Allan	$12.95	Softcover
1-59540-405-8	Tales Of Terror And Mystery	Doyle, Arthur Conan	$13.95	Softcover
1-59540-602-6	Tales of Two Countries	Kielland, Alexander	$11.95	Softcover
1-59540-210-1	Tarzan And The Jewels of Opar	Burroughs, Edgar Rice	$13.95	Softcover
1-4218-0710-6	Tarzan And The Jewels of Opar	Burroughs, Edgar Rice	$28.95	Hardcover
1-59540-211-X	Tarzan of the Apes	Burroughs, Edgar Rice	$15.95	Softcover
1-4218-0711-4	Tarzan of the Apes	Burroughs, Edgar Rice	$31.95	Hardcover
1-59540-212-8	Tarzan the Terrible	Burroughs, Edgar Rice	$15.95	Softcover
1-4218-0712-2	Tarzan the Terrible	Burroughs, Edgar Rice	$31.95	Hardcover
1-59540-213-6	Tarzan the Untamed	Burroughs, Edgar Rice	$17.95	Softcover
1-4218-0713-0	Tarzan the Untamed	Burroughs, Edgar Rice	$33.95	Hardcover
1-4218-1100-6	Tenterhooks	Leverson, Ada	$12.95	Softcover
1-4218-1176-6	The Adventure Club Afloat	Barbour, Ralph Henry	$12.95	Softcover
1-59540-406-6	The Adventures Of Gerard	Doyle, Arthur Conan	$12.95	Softcover
1-4218-1535-4	The Adventures of Harry Richmond, Book 1	Meredith, George	$10.95	Softcover
1-4218-1536-2	The Adventures of Harry Richmond, Book 2	Meredith, George	$10.95	Softcover
1-4218-1537-0	The Adventures of Harry Richmond, Book 3	Meredith, George	$10.95	Softcover
1-4218-1538-9	The Adventures of Harry Richmond, Book 4	Meredith, George	$10.95	Softcover
1-4218-1539-7	The Adventures of Harry Richmond, Book 5	Meredith, George	$10.95	Softcover
1-4218-1540-0	The Adventures of Harry Richmond, Book 6	Meredith, George	$10.95	Softcover
1-4218-1541-9	The Adventures of Harry Richmond, Book 7	Meredith, George	$10.95	Softcover
1-4218-1542-7	The Adventures of Harry Richmond, Book 8	Meredith, George	$10.95	Softcover
1-59540-317-5	The Adventures Of Huckleberry Finn	Twain, Mark	$15.95	Softcover
1-4218-0767-X	The Adventures Of Huckleberry Finn	Twain, Mark	$31.95	Hardcover
1-59540-036-2	The Adventures of Peter Pan	Barrie, J. M.	$12.95	Softcover
1-4218-0636-3	The Adventures of Peter Pan	Barrie, J. M.	$27.95	Hardcover
1-59540-008-7	The Adventures of Pinocchio	Collodi, C.	$12.95	Softcover
1-4218-0608-8	The Adventures of Pinocchio	Collodi, C.	$27.95	Hardcover
1-59540-695-6	The Adventures of Reddy Fox	Burgess, Thornton W.	$10.95	Softcover

ISBN	TITLE	AUTHOR	RETAIL	EDITION
1-59540-407-4	The Adventures Of Sherlock Holmes	Doyle, Arthur Conan	$14.95	Softcover
1-59540-318-3	The Adventures Of Tom Sawyer	Twain, Mark	$13.95	Softcover
1-4218-0768-8	The Adventures Of Tom Sawyer	Twain, Mark	$28.95	Hardcover
1-4218-0494-8	The Allen House	Arthur, T. S.	$14.95	Softcover
1-59540-646-8	The Altar of The Dead	James, Henry	$10.95	Softcover
1-4218-1179-0	The Amateur Poacher	Jefferies, Richard	$11.95	Softcover
1-4218-1527-3	The American Child	Macracken, Elizabeth	$10.95	Softcover
1-59540-319-1	The American Claimant	Twain, Mark	$12.95	Softcover
1-59540-422-8	The Analects	Confucius	$11.95	Softcover
1-59540-614-X	The Ancien Regime	Kingsley, Charles	$10.95	Softcover
1-59540-018-4	The Autobiography of Charles Darwin	Darwin, Francis	$10.95	Softcover
1-4218-0115-9	The Avenger	Oppenheim, E. Phillips	$15.95	Softcover
1-4218-1177-4	The Barrier	Beach, Rex	$14.95	Softcover
1-59540-214-4	The Beasts Of Tarzan	Burroughs, Edgar Rice	$13.95	Softcover
1-4218-0714-9	The Beasts Of Tarzan	Burroughs, Edgar Rice	$28.95	Hardcover
1-4218-0406-9	The Beautiful Lady	Tarkington, Booth	$10.95	Softcover
1-59540-665-4	The Beggar's Opera	Gay, John	$10.95	Softcover
1-4218-0122-1	The Best British Short Stories of 1922	O'Biren, Edward J.	$18.95	Softcover
1-4218-1107-3	The Bishop and Other Stories	Chekhov, Anton	$13.95	Softcover
1-59540-511-9	The Black Arrow	Stevenson, R. L.	$14.95	Softcover
1-4218-0499-9	The Black Dwarf	Scott, Walter	$12.95	Softcover
1-59540-603-4	The Black Tulip	Dumas, Alexandre	$15.95	Softcover
1-4218-0466-2	The Blue Moon	Housman, Laurence	$10.95	Softcover
1-59540-103-2	The Bobbsey Twins at Meadow Brook	Hope, Laura Lee	$12.95	Softcover
1-4218-0653-3	The Bobbsey Twins at Meadow Brook	Hope, Laura Lee	$27.95	Hardcover
1-59540-104-0	The Bobbsey Twins at School	Hope, Laura Lee	$11.95	Softcover
1-4218-0654-1	The Bobbsey Twins at School	Hope, Laura Lee	$26.95	Hardcover
1-59540-673-5	The Bobbsey Twins at Snow Lodge	Hope, Laura Lee	$11.95	Softcover
1-4218-1170-7	The Bobbsey Twins at the Seashore	Hope, Laura Lee	$11.95	Softcover
1-4218-1582-6	The Bobbsey Twins in a Great City	Hope, Laura Lee	$12.95	Softcover
1-59540-105-9	The Bobbsey Twins in the Country	Hope, Laura Lee	$12.95	Softcover

ISBN	TITLE	AUTHOR	RETAIL	EDITION
1-4218-0655-X	The Bobbsey Twins in the Country	Hope, Laura Lee	$27.95	Hardcover
1-4218-0465-4	The Bobbsey Twins in the Great West	Hope, Laura Lee	$12.95	Softcover
1-59540-674-3	The Bobbsey Twins in Washington	Hope, Laura Lee	$12.95	Softcover
1-4218-1167-7	The Bobbsey Twins on A House Boat	Hope, Laura Lee	$12.95	Softcover
1-59540-127-X	The Book of Snobs	Thackeray, William Makepeace	$13.95	Softcover
1-4218-0677-0	The Book of Snobs	Thackeray, William Makepeace	$28.95	Hardcover
1-59540-045-1	The Book of Tea	Okakura, Kakuzo	$10.95	Softcover
1-59540-535-6	The Border Legion	Grey, Zane	$15.95	Softcover
1-4218-0885-4	The Border Legion	Grey, Zane	$31.95	Hardcover
1-4218-0484-0	The Boy Allies at Jutland	Drake, Robert L.	$13.95	Softcover
1-4218-0424-7	The Boy Allies at Verdun	Hayes, Clair W.	$13.95	Softcover
1-4218-1183-9	The Boy Allies Under the Sea	Drake, Robert L.	$12.95	Softcover
1-4218-0483-2	The Boy Allies Under Two Flags	Drake, Robert L.	$13.95	Softcover
1-4218-1182-0	The Boy Allies with the Victorious Fleets	Drake, Robert L.	$12.95	Softcover
1-4218-1181-2	The Boy Allies with Uncle Sams Cruisers	Drake, Robert L.	$12.95	Softcover
1-59540-816-9	The Boy Aviators in Africa	Lawton, Wilbur	$12.95	Softcover
1-4218-1195-2	The Boy Aviators' Treasure Quest	Lawton, Wilbur	$12.95	Softcover
1-4218-1140-5	The Boy Knight	Henty, G.A.	$14.95	Softcover
1-4218-0435-2	The Boy Life of Napoleon	Foa, Eugenie	$11.95	Softcover
1-59540-808-8	The Boy Ranchers on the Trail	Baker, Willard F.	$12.95	Softcover
1-4218-1532-X	The Boy Scout Aviators	Durston, George	$10.95	Softcover
1-4218-1533-8	The Boy Scouts in front of Warsaw	Durston, George	$10.95	Softcover
1-59540-434-1	The Boys Life of Abraham Lincoln	Nicolay, Helen	$11.95	Softcover
1-4218-0156-6	The Bride of The Mistletoe	Allen, James Lane	$10.95	Softcover
1-59540-820-7	The Brighton Boys with the Flying Corps	Driscoll, James R.	$11.95	Softcover
1-59540-821-5	The Brighton Boys with the Submarine Fleet	Driscoll, James R.	$11.95	Softcover
1-4218-0136-1	The British Barbarians	Allen, Grant	$10.95	Softcover
1-4218-0103-5	The Brown Fairy Book	Lang, Andrew	$15.95	Softcover
1-59540-696-4	The Burgess Animal Book for Children	Burgess, Thornton W.	$14.95	Softcover
1-59540-666-2	The Burning Spear	Glasworthy, John	$12.95	Softcover

ISBN	TITLE	AUTHOR	RETAIL	EDITION
1-59540-694-8	The Caesars	Quincey, Thomas De	$12.95	Softcover
1-59540-536-4	The Call Of The Canyon	Grey, Zane	$13.95	Softcover
1-4218-0886-2	The Call Of The Canyon	Grey, Zane	$28.95	Hardcover
1-4218-0490-5	The Call of the North	White, Stewart Edward	$11.95	Softcover
1-59540-039-7	The Call of the Wild	London, Jack	$10.95	Softcover
1-4218-0639-8	The Call of the Wild	London, Jack	$26.95	Hardcover
1-59540-677-8	The Camp Fire Girls at Sunrise Hill	Vandercook, Margaret	$11.95	Softcover
1-59540-408-2	The Captain Of The Polestar	Doyle, Arthur Conan	$14.95	Softcover
1-4218-0145-0	The Cash Boy	Alger Jr., Horatio	$11.95	Softcover
1-4218-0454-9	The Castle of Otranto	Walpole, Horace	$10.95	Softcover
1-59540-657-3	The Cathedral	Walpole, Hugh	$21.95	Softcover
1-4218-1543-5	The Cavalier	Cable, George W.	$14.95	Softcover
1-59540-134-2	The Celebrity	Churchill, Winston	$12.95	Softcover
1-59540-647-6	The Chaperon	James, Henry	$10.95	Softcover
1-59540-215-2	The Chessmen of Mars	Burroughs, Edgar Rice	$14.95	Softcover
1-4218-0715-7	The Chessmen of Mars	Burroughs, Edgar Rice	$29.95	Hardcover
1-4218-0460-3	The Choir Invisible	Allen, James Lane	$13.95	Softcover
1-4218-1120-0	The Circus Boys Across The Continent	Darlington, Edgar B.P.	$12.95	Softcover
1-4218-1121-9	The Circus Boys In Dixie Land	Darlington, Edgar B.P.	$12.95	Softcover
1-4218-1122-7	The Circus Boys on the Flying Rings	Darlington, Edgar B.P.	$12.95	Softcover
1-4218-1123-5	The Circus Boys On the Mississippi	Darlington, Edgar B.P.	$12.95	Softcover
1-59540-651-4	The Civilization of China	Giles, Herbert A.	$11.95	Softcover
1-59540-435-X	The Cleveland Era	Ford, Henry Jones	$11.95	Softcover
1-59540-342-6	The Clicking Of Cuthbert	Wodehouse, P. G.	$13.95	Softcover
1-4218-0792-0	The Clicking Of Cuthbert	Wodehouse, P. G.	$28.95	Hardcover
1-4218-0439-5	The Collectors	Mather, Frank Jewett	$10.95	Softcover
1-59540-343-4	The Coming Of Bill	Wodehouse, P. G.	$15.95	Softcover
1-4218-0793-9	The Coming Of Bill	Wodehouse, P. G.	$31.95	Hardcover
1-4218-0189-2	The Coming of Cuculain	O'Grady, Standish	$10.95	Softcover
1-59540-011-7	The Complete Works Of Artemus Ward , Part 3	Browne, Charles Farrar	$10.95	Softcover
1-59540-448-1	The Conduct Of Life	Emerson, Ralph Waldo	$12.95	Softcover
1-4218-0848-X	The Conduct Of Life	Emerson, Ralph Waldo	$27.95	Hardcover
1-59540-612-3	The Conquest of Fear	King, Basil	$12.95	Softcover

ISBN	TITLE	AUTHOR	RETAIL	EDITION
1-4218-0912-5	The Conquest of Fear	King, Basil	$27.95	Hardcover
1-59540-620-4	The Consolidator	Defoe, Daniel	$12.95	Softcover
1-59540-675-1	The Cossacks	Tolstoy, Leo	$13.95	Softcover
1-4218-0975-3	The Cossacks	Tolstoy, Leo	$28.95	Hardcover
1-4218-1132-4	The Covered Wagon	Hough, Emerson	$14.95	Softcover
1-4218-0106-X	The Crimson Fairy Book	Lang, Andrew	$15.95	Softcover
1-59540-135-0	The Crisis	Churchill, Winston	$26.95	Softcover
1-4218-0685-1	The Crisis	Churchill, Winston	$45.95	Hardcover
1-59540-609-3	The Crisis in Russia	Ransome, Arthur	$10.95	Softcover
1-4218-1168-5	The Crushed Flower and Other Stories	Andreyev, Leonid	$14.95	Softcover
1-4218-1566-4	The Curlytops at Uncle Franks Ranch	Garis, Howard R.	$11.95	Softcover
1-4218-1567-2	The Curlytops on Star Island	Garis, Howard R.	$11.95	Softcover
1-4218-1612-1	The Czar's Spy	Le Queux, William	$14.95	Softcover
1-4218-0472-7	The Daredevil	Daviess, Maria Thompson	$12.95	Softcover
1-59540-809-6	The Delicious Vice	Allison, Young E.	$10.95	Softcover
1-59540-653-0	The Deserted Woman	Balzac, Honore De	$10.95	Softcover
1-59540-300-0	The Devil's Disciple	Shaw, George Bernard	$10.95	Softcover
1-4218-0750-5	The Devil's Disciple	Shaw, George Bernard	$26.95	Hardcover
1-4218-0116-7	The Devil's Paw	Oppenheim, E. Phillips	$13.95	Softcover
1-59540-301-9	The Doctor's Dilemma	Shaw, George Bernard	$11.95	Softcover
1-4218-0751-3	The Doctor's Dilemma	Shaw, George Bernard	$26.95	Hardcover
1-4218-1108-1	The Duel and Other Stories	Chekhov, Anton	$13.95	Softcover
1-59540-136-9	The Dwelling-Place of Light, Vol 1	Churchill, Winston	$11.95	Softcover
1-59540-137-7	The Dwelling-Place of Light, Vol 2	Churchill, Winston	$11.95	Softcover
1-59540-138-5	The Dwelling-Place of Light, Vol 3	Churchill, Winston	$11.95	Softcover
1-59540-512-7	The Dynamiter	Stevenson, R. L.	$13.95	Softcover
1-4218-0862-5	The Dynamiter	Stevenson, R. L.	$28.95	Hardcover
1-59540-513-5	The Ebb Tide	Stevenson, R. L.	$11.95	Softcover
1-4218-0863-3	The Ebb Tide	Stevenson, R. L.	$26.95	Hardcover
1-59540-628-X	The Education of the Child	Key, Ellen	$10.95	Softcover
1-59540-216-0	The Efficiency Expert	Burroughs, Edgar Rice	$12.95	Softcover
1-4218-0716-5	The Efficiency Expert	Burroughs, Edgar Rice	$27.95	Hardcover

ISBN	TITLE	AUTHOR	RETAIL	EDITION
1-4218-0131-0	The Elect Lady	MacDonald, George	$13.95	Softcover
1-4218-0109-4	The Elusive Pimpernel	Orczy, Baroness Emmuska	$15.95	Softcover
1-4218-0009-8	The Elusive Pimpernel	Orczy, Baroness Emmuska	$31.95	Hardcover
1-4218-0464-6	The Emerald City of Oz	Baum, L. Frank	$13.95	Softcover
1-4218-1580-X	The Enchanted Island of Yew	Baum, L. Frank	$11.95	Softcover
1-4218-1574-5	The Enchanted Typewriter	Bangs, John Kendrick	$10.95	Softcover
1-4218-0455-7	The Errand Boy	Alger Jr., Horatio	$14.95	Softcover
1-59540-648-4	The Europeans	James, Henry	$12.95	Softcover
1-4218-0948-6	The Europeans	James, Henry	$27.95	Hardcover
1-4218-0117-5	The Evil Shepherd	Oppenheim, E. Phillips	$14.95	Softcover
1-59540-668-9	The Fifth String	Sousa, John Philip	$10.95	Softcover
1-4218-0178-7	The Firefly of France	Angellotti, Marion Polk	$13.95	Softcover
1-59540-636-0	The First Men In The Moon	Wells, H. G.	$13.95	Softcover
1-4218-0936-2	The First Men In The Moon	Wells, H. G.	$28.95	Hardcover
1-4218-0157-4	The Flaming Forest	Curwood, James Oliver	$13.95	Softcover
1-4218-0132-9	The Flight of the Shadow	MacDonald, George	$13.95	Softcover
1-59540-622-0	The Flying Saucers are Real	Keyhole, Donald	$13.95	Softcover
1-4218-0922-2	The Flying Saucers are Real	Keyhole, Donald	$28.95	Hardcover
1-4218-1173-1	The Fortieth Door	Bradley, Mary Hastings	$13.95	Softcover
1-4218-1197-9	The Four Faces	Queux, William le	$14.95	Softcover
1-59540-635-2	The Fourth Watch	Cody, H. A.	$14.95	Softcover
1-4218-1577-X	The Free Rangers	Altsheler, Joseph A.	$14.95	Softcover
1-59540-608-5	The Freedom of Life	Call, Annie Payson	$10.95	Softcover
1-4218-0128-0	The Gambler	Dostoyevsky, Fyodor	$12.95	Softcover
1-4218-0101-9	The Gentleman	Ollivant, Alfred	$15.95	Softcover
1-4218-0113-2	The Ghost of Guir House	Willing, Charles	$11.95	Softcover
1-4218-0453-0	The Girl with the Golden Eyes	Balzac, Honore de	$10.95	Softcover
1-59540-690-5	The Go Ahead Boy and the Racing Motor-Boat	Kay, Ross	$12.95	Softcover
1-4218-0411-5	The Gold Bag	Wells, Carolyn	$13.95	Softcover
1-59540-344-2	The Gold Bat	Wodehouse, P. G.	$12.95	Softcover
1-4218-0794-7	The Gold Bat	Wodehouse, P. G.	$27.95	Hardcover
1-59540-002-8	The Goodness of St.Rocque	Dunbar, Alice	$10.95	Softcover
1-4218-0404-2	The Grand Babylon Hotel	Bennett, Arnold	$14.95	Softcover
1-59540-409-0	The Great Boer War	Doyle, Arthur Conan	$26.95	Softcover

ISBN	TITLE	AUTHOR	RETAIL	EDITION
1-4218-0118-3	The Great Impersonation	Oppenheim, E. Phillips	$14.95	Softcover
1-4218-0018-7	The Great Impersonation	Oppenheim, E. Phillips	$29.95	Hardcover
1-4218-0119-1	The Great Secret	Oppenheim, E. Phillips	$15.95	Softcover
1-59540-113-X	The Great Stone Face	Hawthorne, Nathaniel	$10.95	Softcover
1-4218-1546-X	The Great Taboo	Allen, Grant	$13.95	Softcover
1-4218-1594-X	The Half-Back	Barbour, Ralph Henry	$12.95	Softcover
1-4218-0102-7	The Happiest Time of Their Lives	Miller, Alice Duer	$13.95	Softcover
1-4218-0172-8	The Happy Adventures	Middleton, Lydia Miller	$13.95	Softcover
1-4218-1114-6	The Happy Family	Bower, Bertha Muzzy	$12.95	Softcover
1-4218-1133-2	The Happy Foreigner	Bagnold, Enid	$12.95	Softcover
1-59540-697-2	The Haunted Hotel	Collins, Wilkie	$13.95	Softcover
1-4218-0997-4	The Haunted Hotel	Collins, Wilkie	$28.95	Hardcover
1-4218-0426-3	The Head Hunters of Northern Luzon	Willcox, Cornelis DeWitt	$12.95	Softcover
1-59540-345-0	The Head Of Kay's	Wodehouse, P. G.	$11.95	Softcover
1-4218-0795-5	The Head Of Kay's	Wodehouse, P. G.	$26.95	Hardcover
1-59540-537-2	The Heritage Of The Desert	Grey, Zane	$14.95	Softcover
1-4218-0887-0	The Heritage Of The Desert	Grey, Zane	$29.95	Hardcover
1-59540-615-8	The Hermits	Kingsley, Charles	$14.95	Softcover
1-4218-0450-6	The High School Boy's Training Hike	Hancock, H. Irving	$12.95	Softcover
1-4218-1142-1	The Highwayman	Bailey, H.C.	$14.95	Softcover
1-4218-0427-1	The Hilltop Boys on the River	Burleigh, Cyril	$11.95	Softcover
1-59540-652-2	The History of The Telephone	Casson, Herbert N.	$11.95	Softcover
1-59540-410-4	The Hound Of Baskervilles	Doyle, Arthur Conan	$12.95	Softcover
1-4218-0810-2	The Hound Of Baskervilles	Doyle, Arthur Conan	$27.95	Hardcover
1-59540-683-2	The House of The Seven Gables	Hawthorne, Nathaniel	$15.95	Softcover
1-59540-663-8	The Hunchback	Knowles, James Sheridan	$10.95	Softcover
1-4218-0481-6	The Hungry Stones	Tagore, Rabindranath	$12.95	Softcover
1-4218-0486-7	The Idol of Paris	Bernhardt, Sarah	$14.95	Softcover
1-4218-1519-2	The Illustrious Prince	Oppenheim, E. Phillips	$15.95	Softcover
1-59540-693-X	The Imitation of Christ	Kempis, Thomas A	$14.95	Softcover
1-4218-0993-1	The Imitation of Christ	Kempis, Thomas A	$29.95	Hardcover
1-59540-114-8	The Importance of being Earnest	Wilde, Oscar	$10.95	Softcover
1-4218-0664-9	The Importance of being Earnest	Wilde, Oscar	$26.95	Hardcover

ISBN	TITLE	AUTHOR	RETAIL	EDITION
1-4218-1547-8	The Inferno	Barbusse, Henri	$11.95	Softcover
1-4218-1581-8	The Inn at the Red Oak	Griswold, Latta	$12.95	Softcover
1-4218-1113-8	The Inner Shrine	King, Basil	$13.95	Softcover
1-59540-139-3	The Inside of The Cup Vol 1.	Churchill, Winston	$10.95	Softcover
1-59540-140-7	The Inside of The Cup Vol 2.	Churchill, Winston	$10.95	Softcover
1-59540-141-5	The Inside of The Cup Vol 3.	Churchill, Winston	$10.95	Softcover
1-59540-142-3	The Inside of The Cup Vol 4.	Churchill, Winston	$10.95	Softcover
1-59540-143-1	The Inside of The Cup Vol 5.	Churchill, Winston	$10.95	Softcover
1-59540-144-X	The Inside of The Cup Vol 6.	Churchill, Winston	$10.95	Softcover
1-59540-145-8	The Inside of The Cup Vol 7.	Churchill, Winston	$10.95	Softcover
1-59540-146-6	The Inside of The Cup Vol 8.	Churchill, Winston	$10.95	Softcover
1-59540-346-9	The Intrusion Of Jimmy	Wodehouse, P. G.	$14.95	Softcover
1-4218-0796-3	The Intrusion Of Jimmy	Wodehouse, P. G.	$29.95	Hardcover
1-59540-028-1	The Island of Doctor Moreau	Wells, H. G.	$11.95	Softcover
1-4218-0628-2	The Island of Doctor Moreau	Wells, H. G.	$26.95	Hardcover
1-4218-0470-0	The Island of Faith	Sangster, Margaret E.	$10.95	Softcover
1-4218-0140-X	The Isle of Unrest	Merriman, Henry Seton	$14.95	Softcover
1-4218-0469-7	The Japanese Twins	Perkins, Lucy Fitch	$10.95	Softcover
1-4218-1148-0	The Jew and other stories	Turgenev, Ivan	$13.95	Softcover
1-4218-0111-6	The Jewel City	Macomber, Ben	$12.95	Softcover
1-59540-007-9	The Jewel of Seven Stars	Stoker, Bram	$14.95	Softcover
1-4218-0607-X	The Jewel of Seven Stars	Stoker, Bram	$29.95	Hardcover
1-59540-517-8	The Jungle Book	Kipling, Rudyard	$12.95	Softcover
1-4218-0867-6	The Jungle Book	Kipling, Rudyard	$27.95	Hardcover
1-59540-217-9	The Jungle Tales Of Tarzan	Burroughs, Edgar Rice	$13.95	Softcover
1-4218-0717-3	The Jungle Tales Of Tarzan	Burroughs, Edgar Rice	$28.95	Hardcover
1-4218-0120-5	The Kingdom of The Blind	Oppenheim, E. Phillips	$14.95	Softcover
1-4218-0420-4	The Lances of Lynwood	Yonge, Charlotte M.	$12.95	Softcover
1-59540-679-4	The Land of Little Rain	Austin, Mary	$10.95	Softcover
1-4218-0979-6	The Land of Little Rain	Austin, Mary	$26.95	Hardcover
1-59540-218-7	The Land that Time Forgot	Burroughs, Edgar Rice	$10.95	Softcover
1-59540-538-0	The Last Of The Plainsman	Grey, Zane	$13.95	Softcover
1-4218-0888-9	The Last Of The Plainsman	Grey, Zane	$28.95	Hardcover
1-4218-1131-6	The Law of the Land	Hough, Emerson	$13.95	Softcover
1-59540-126-1	The Legend of Sleepy Hollow	Irving, Washington	$10.95	Softcover
1-59540-202-0	The Letters of Anton Chekhov	Chekhov, Anton	$20.95	Softcover

ISBN	TITLE	AUTHOR	RETAIL	EDITION
1-4218-0702-5	The Letters of Anton Chekhov	Chekhov, Anton	$37.95	Hardcover
1-59540-320-5	The Letters Of Mark Twain Vol.1	Twain, Mark	$11.95	Softcover
1-59540-321-3	The Letters Of Mark Twain Vol.2	Twain, Mark	$12.95	Softcover
1-59540-322-1	The Letters Of Mark Twain Vol.3	Twain, Mark	$13.95	Softcover
1-59540-323-X	The Letters Of Mark Twain Vol.4	Twain, Mark	$14.95	Softcover
1-59540-324-8	The Letters Of Mark Twain Vol.5 & 6	Twain, Mark	$12.95	Softcover
1-4218-1531-1	The Life and Adventures of Santa Clause	Baum, L. Frank	$10.95	Softcover
1-59540-623-9	The Life and Perambulations of a Mouse	Kilner, Dorothy	$10.95	Softcover
1-59540-539-9	The Light Of The Western Stars	Grey, Zane	$18.95	Softcover
1-4218-0889-7	The Light Of The Western Stars	Grey, Zane	$35.95	Hardcover
1-4218-1175-8	The Light That Lures	Brebner, Percy	$14.95	Softcover
1-4218-0105-1	The Lilac Fairy Book	Lang, Andrew	$15.95	Softcover
1-4218-1595-8	The Lilac Girl	Barbour, Ralph Henry	$10.95	Softcover
1-4218-1117-0	The Lion and the Mouse	Klein, Charles	$13.95	Softcover
1-4218-0418-2	The Little Duke	Yonge, Charlotte M.	$11.95	Softcover
1-59540-347-7	The Little Nugget	Wodehouse, P. G.	$14.95	Softcover
1-4218-0797-1	The Little Nugget	Wodehouse, P. G.	$29.95	Hardcover
1-59540-348-5	The Little Warrior	Wodehouse, P. G.	$20.95	Softcover
1-59540-671-9	The Lock and Key Library	Hawthrone, Julian	$13.95	Softcover
1-4218-0162-0	The Lock And Key Library Classic Mystrey and Detective Stories	Hawthrone, Julian	$18.95	Softcover
1-59540-540-2	The Lone Star Ranger	Grey, Zane	$15.95	Softcover
1-4218-0890-0	The Lone Star Ranger	Grey, Zane	$31.95	Hardcover
1-59540-684-0	The Long Chance	Kyne, Peter B.	$15.95	Softcover
1-4218-1155-3	The Lost City	Badger Jr., Joseph E.	$12.95	Softcover
1-59540-219-5	The Lost Continent	Burroughs, Edgar Rice	$11.95	Softcover
1-59540-047-8	The Lost Princess of Oz	Baum, L. Frank	$12.95	Softcover
1-4218-0647-9	The Lost Princess of Oz	Baum, L. Frank	$27.95	Hardcover
1-59540-411-2	The Lost World	Doyle, Arthur Conan	$13.95	Softcover
1-4218-0811-0	The Lost World	Doyle, Arthur Conan	$28.95	Hardcover
1-59540-220-9	The Mad King	Burroughs, Edgar Rice	$15.95	Softcover
1-59540-101-6	The Magic of Oz	Baum, L. Frank	$11.95	Softcover

ISBN	TITLE	AUTHOR	RETAIL	EDITION
1-4218-0651-7	The Magic of Oz	Baum, L. Frank	$26.95	Hardcover
1-4218-1520-6	The Malefactor	Oppenheim, E. Phillips	$15.95	Softcover
1-59540-658-1	The Man From The Clouds	Clouston, J. Storer	$13.95	Softcover
1-4218-0463-8	The Man in Lonely Land	Bosher, Kate Langley	$11.95	Softcover
1-59540-541-0	The Man Of The Forest	Grey, Zane	$20.95	Softcover
1-4218-0891-9	The Man Of The Forest	Grey, Zane	$37.95	Hardcover
1-4218-0138-8	The Man on the Box	McGrath, Harold	$14.95	Softcover
1-59540-325-6	The Man That Corrupted Hadleyburg	Twain, Mark	$18.95	Softcover
1-4218-0775-0	The Man That Corrupted Hadleyburg	Twain, Mark	$35.95	Hardcover
1-4218-1550-8	The Marriage Contract	De Balzac, Honore	$11.95	Softcover
1-59540-526-7	The Martin Luther King Jr	Various Authors	$18.95	Softcover
1-59540-100-8	The Marvelous Land of Oz	Baum, L. Frank	$12.95	Softcover
1-4218-0650-9	The Marvelous Land of Oz	Baum, L. Frank	$27.95	Hardcover
1-4218-0457-3	The Mason-Bees	Fabre, J Henri	$12.95	Softcover
1-4218-1158-8	The Masquerader	Thurston, Katherine Cecil	$15.95	Softcover
1-4218-1147-2	The Master of Silence	Bacheller, Irving	$10.95	Softcover
1-59540-522-4	The Mayor Of Casterbridge	Hardy, Thomas	$17.95	Softcover
1-4218-0872-2	The Mayor Of Casterbridge	Hardy, Thomas	$33.95	Hardcover
1-59540-655-7	The Merry Adventures of Robin Hood	Pyle, Howard	$17.95	Softcover
1-59540-514-3	The Merry Men	Stevenson, R. L.	$14.95	Softcover
1-4218-0864-1	The Merry Men	Stevenson, R. L.	$29.95	Hardcover
1-4218-1149-9	The Middle of Things	Fletcher, J.S.	$13.95	Softcover
1-4218-0159-0	The Minute Boys of Mohawk Valley	Otis, James	$14.95	Softcover
1-4218-0121-3	The Mischief-Maker	Oppenheim, E. Phillips	$17.95	Softcover
1-59540-221-7	The Monster Men	Burroughs, Edgar Rice	$12.95	Softcover
1-4218-0441-7	The Moon Metal	Serviss, Garrett P.	$10.95	Softcover
1-4218-1588-5	The Motor Girls	Penrose, Margret	$12.95	Softcover
1-4218-1590-7	The Motor Girls on a Tour	Penrose, Margret	$12.95	Softcover
1-4218-1589-3	The Motor Girls on Cedar Lake	Penrose, Margret	$12.95	Softcover
1-4218-1159-6	The Motor Maids in Fair Japan	Stokes, Katherine	$12.95	Softcover
1-4218-0171-X	The Motormaniacs	Osbourne, Lloyd	$10.95	Softcover
1-4218-0491-3	The Mountains	White, Stewart Edward	$12.95	Softcover
1-4218-1599-0	The Moving Picture Boys at Panama	Appleton, Victor	$12.95	Softcover

ISBN	TITLE	AUTHOR	RETAIL	EDITION
1-59540-222-5	The Mucker	Burroughs, Edgar Rice	$20.95	Softcover
1-59540-601-8	The Mysterious Affair at Styles	Christie, Agatha	$13.95	Softcover
1-59540-326-4	The Mysterious Stranger	Twain, Mark	$11.95	Softcover
1-4218-0776-9	The Mysterious Stranger	Twain, Mark	$26.95	Hardcover
1-59540-427-9	The Narrative Of Arthur Gordon	Poe, Edgar Allan	$13.95	Softcover
1-4218-1139-1	The New Jerusalem	Cherston, G.K.	$13.95	Softcover
1-59540-207-1	The New Revelation	Doyle, Arthur Conan	$10.95	Softcover
1-4218-0158-2	The Nine-Tenths	Oppenheim, James	$14.95	Softcover
1-59540-223-3	The Oakdale Affair	Burroughs, Edgar Rice	$11.95	Softcover
1-4218-1135-9	The Old Gray Homestead	Keyes, Frances Parkinson	$12.95	Softcover
1-4218-0110-8	The Old Man in the Corner	Orczy, Baroness	$13.95	Softcover
1-4218-0125-6	The Old Northwest	Ogg, Federick Austin	$11.95	Softcover
1-59540-688-3	The Open Air	Jefferies, Richard	$13.95	Softcover
1-4218-1150-2	The Orange-Yellow Diamond	Fletcher, J.S.	$13.95	Softcover
1-4218-1163-4	The Outdoor Girls at Rainbow Lake	Hope, Laura Lee	$11.95	Softcover
1-4218-1162-6	The Outdoor Girls at the Hostess House	Hope, Laura Lee	$11.95	Softcover
1-4218-1160-X	The Outdoor Girls at Wild Rose Lodge	Hope, Laura Lee	$11.95	Softcover
1-4218-1161-8	The Outdoor Girls in Army Service	Hope, Laura Lee	$11.95	Softcover
1-4218-1164-2	The Outdoor Girls of Deepdale	Hope, Laura Lee	$11.95	Softcover
1-59540-224-1	The Outlaw of Torn	Burroughs, Edgar Rice	$13.95	Softcover
1-4218-1106-5	The Outlet	Adams, Andy	$13.95	Softcover
1-59540-699-9	The Pastor's Son	Walter, William W.	$10.95	Softcover
1-59540-630-1	The Path of A Star	Cotes, Everard	$14.95	Softcover
1-4218-0493-X	The Path of Life	Streuvels, Stijn	$11.95	Softcover
1-4218-0184-1	The Peace Negotiations	Lansing, Robert	$14.95	Softcover
1-4218-1571-0	The People of the Abyss	London, Jack	$13.95	Softcover
1-59540-302-7	The Perfect Wagnerite	Shaw, George Bernard	$11.95	Softcover
1-4218-0752-1	The Perfect Wagnerite	Shaw, George Bernard	$26.95	Hardcover
1-59540-124-5	The Personal Memoirs of U.S. Grant, Vol 1.	Grant, U. S.	$18.95	Softcover
1-4218-0674-6	The Personal Memoirs of U.S. Grant, Vol 1.	Grant, U. S.	$35.95	Hardcover
1-59540-125-3	The Personal Memoirs of U.S. Grant, Vol 2.	Grant, U. S.	$21.95	Softcover

ISBN	TITLE	AUTHOR	RETAIL	EDITION
1-4218-0675-4	The Personal Memoirs of U.S. Grant, Vol 2.	Grant, U. S.	$39.95	Hardcover
1-4218-0405-0	The Phantom Herd	Bower, B. M.	$13.95	Softcover
1-59540-024-9	The Phantom of the Opera	Leroux, Gaston	$15.95	Softcover
1-4218-0624-X	The Phantom of the Opera	Leroux, Gaston	$31.95	Hardcover
1-59540-303-5	The Philanderer	Shaw, George Bernard	$10.95	Softcover
1-4218-0753-X	The Philanderer	Shaw, George Bernard	$26.95	Hardcover
1-59540-338-8	The Picture Of Dorian Gray	Wilde, Oscar	$12.95	Softcover
1-4218-0788-2	The Picture Of Dorian Gray	Wilde, Oscar	$27.95	Hardcover
1-4218-0104-3	The Pink Fairy Book	Lang, Andrew	$15.95	Softcover
1-4218-1184-7	The Pleasures of Ignorance	Lynd, Robert	$11.95	Softcover
1-59540-412-0	The Poison Belt	Doyle, Arthur Conan	$10.95	Softcover
1-4218-0812-9	The Poison Belt	Doyle, Arthur Conan	$26.95	Hardcover
1-4218-1529-X	The Pony Rider Boys in New Mexico	Patchin, Frank G.	$13.95	Softcover
1-4218-0437-9	The Pony Rider Boys in the Grand Canyon	Patchin, Frank Gee	$12.95	Softcover
1-4218-1530-3	The Pony Rider Boys in the Ozarks	Patchin, Frank G.	$13.95	Softcover
1-4218-0438-7	The Pony Rider Boys with The Texas Rangers	Patchin, Frank Gee	$12.95	Softcover
1-4218-1143-X	The Poor Gentleman	Conscience, Hendrick	$10.95	Softcover
1-4218-0468-9	The Postmaster's Daughter	Tracy, Louis	$14.95	Softcover
1-4218-1174-X	The Prince	Machiavelli, Nicolo	$11.95	Softcover
1-59540-327-2	The Prince And The Pauper	Twain, Mark	$14.95	Softcover
1-4218-0777-7	The Prince And The Pauper	Twain, Mark	$29.95	Hardcover
1-4218-0440-9	The Principles of Scientific Management	Taylor, Frederick Winslow	$10.95	Softcover
1-59540-649-2	The Pupil	James, Henry	$10.95	Softcover
1-4218-1575-3	The Pursuit of the House-Boat	Bangs, John Kendrick	$10.95	Softcover
1-4218-1598-2	The Queen of Sheba & My Cousin the Colonel	Aldrich, Thomad Bailey	$12.95	Softcover
1-59540-542-9	The Rainbow Trail	Grey, Zane	$15.95	Softcover
1-4218-0892-7	The Rainbow Trail	Grey, Zane	$31.95	Hardcover
1-4218-1110-3	The Range Dwellers	Bower, B. M.	$10.95	Softcover
1-59540-119-9	The Red Badge of Courage	Crane, Stephen	$11.95	Softcover
1-4218-0669-X	The Red Badge of Courage	Crane, Stephen	$26.95	Hardcover
1-59540-687-5	The Red Cross Girl	Davis, Richard Harding	$13.95	Softcover
1-59540-543-7	The Redheaded Outfield	Grey, Zane	$12.95	Softcover

ISBN	TITLE	AUTHOR	RETAIL	EDITION
1-4218-1573-7	The Reign of Law	Allen, James Lane	$13.95	Softcover
1-59540-413-9	The Return Of Sherlock Holmes	Doyle, Arthur Conan	$17.95	Softcover
1-59540-225-X	The Return Of Tarzan	Burroughs, Edgar Rice	$15.95	Softcover
1-4218-0165-5	The Road to Oz	Baum, L. Frank	$11.95	Softcover
1-4218-1109-X	The Rover Boys In The Mountains	Winfield, Arthur M.	$12.95	Softcover
1-59540-611-5	The Scarlet Pimpernel	Orczy, Baroness	$15.95	Softcover
1-4218-0911-7	The Scarlet Pimpernel	Orczy, Baroness	$31.95	Hardcover
1-59540-203-9	The School Mistress	Chekhov, Anton	$13.95	Softcover
1-4218-0415-8	The Schoolbook of Forestry	Pack, Charles Lathrop	$10.95	Softcover
1-4218-1154-5	The Scouts of the Valley	Altsheler, Joseph A.	$14.95	Softcover
1-59540-204-7	The Sea-Gull	Chekhov, Anton	$10.95	Softcover
1-4218-0442-5	The Second Deluge	Serviss, Garrett P.	$15.95	Softcover
1-4218-1103-0	The Secret Adversary	Christie, Agatha	$15.95	Softcover
1-59540-019-2	The Secret Garden	Burnett, Frances Hodgson	$14.95	Softcover
1-4218-0619-3	The Secret Garden	Burnett, Frances Hodgson	$29.95	Hardcover
1-4218-0168-X	The Seven Who Were Hanged	Andreyev, Leonid	$10.95	Softcover
1-4218-0477-8	The Sheridan Road Mystery	Thorne, Paul and Mabel	$12.95	Softcover
1-59540-414-7	The Sign Of Four	Doyle, Arthur Conan	$11.95	Softcover
1-4218-0814-5	The Sign Of Four	Doyle, Arthur Conan	$26.95	Hardcover
1-4218-0129-9	The Slim Princess	Ade, George	$10.95	Softcover
1-4218-0124-8	The Solitary Summer	Von Arnim, Elizabeth	$10.95	Softcover
1-4218-0024-1	The Solitary Summer	Von Arnim, Elizabeth	$26.95	Hardcover
1-59540-226-8	The Son Of Tarzan	Burroughs, Edgar Rice	$15.95	Softcover
1-4218-0726-2	The Son Of Tarzan	Burroughs, Edgar Rice	$31.95	Hardcover
1-59540-035-4	The Song of Hiawatha	Longfellow, Henry Wadsworth	$11.95	Softcover
1-4218-0635-5	The Song of Hiawatha	Longfellow, Henry Wadsworth	$26.95	Hardcover
1-4218-1579-6	The Sorrows of a Show Girl	McGaffey, Kenneth	$10.95	Softcover
1-59540-544-5	The Spirit Of The Border	Grey, Zane	$15.95	Softcover
1-4218-0894-3	The Spirit Of The Border	Grey, Zane	$31.95	Hardcover
1-59540-415-5	The Stark Munro Letters	Doyle, Arthur Conan	$13.95	Softcover
1-4218-0495-6	The Stillwater Tragedy	Aldrich, Thomas Bailey	$13.95	Softcover
1-4218-0419-0	The Stokesley Secret	Yonge, Charlotte M.	$13.95	Softcover
1-59540-654-9	The Store Boy	Alger Jr., Horatio	$13.95	Softcover

ISBN	TITLE	AUTHOR	RETAIL	EDITION
1-4218-0954-0	The Store Boy	Alger Jr., Horatio	$28.95	Hardcover
1-4218-0154-X	The Stories Mother Nature Told Her Children	Andrews, James	$10.95	Softcover
1-4218-0199-X	The Story Of A Bad Boy	Aldrich, Thomas Bailey	$12.95	Softcover
1-4218-0099-3	The Story Of A Bad Boy	Aldrich, Thomas Bailey	$27.95	Hardcover
1-4218-0192-2	The Story of Creation	Ackland, T. S.	$11.95	Softcover
1-4218-0147-7	The Story of Doctor Dolittle	Lofting, Hugh	$10.95	Softcover
1-4218-1152-9	The Story of Siegfried	Baldwin, James	$13.95	Softcover
1-59540-116-4	The Strange Case of Dr.Jekyll and Mr Hyde	Stevenson, R. L.	$10.95	Softcover
1-4218-1578-8	The Subterranean Brotherhood	Hawthrone, Julian	$13.95	Softcover
1-59540-624-7	The Theology of Holiness	Clark, Dougan	$10.95	Softcover
1-4218-1515-X	The Thunder Bird	Bower, B. M.	$13.95	Softcover
1-59540-029-X	The Time Machine	Wells, H. G.	$10.95	Softcover
1-4218-0629-0	The Time Machine	Wells, H. G.	$26.95	Hardcover
1-59540-328-0	The Tragedy of Pudd'nhead Wilson	Twain, Mark	$12.95	Softcover
1-4218-0188-4	The Treasure	Lagerlof, Selma	$10.95	Softcover
1-4218-1119-7	The Trespasser	Lawrence, D.H.	$13.95	Softcover
1-59540-642-5	The Triple Alliance	Avery, Harold	$14.95	Softcover
1-59540-523-2	The Trumpet Major	Hardy, Thomas	$18.95	Softcover
1-59540-650-6	The Turn of the Screw	James, Henry	$11.95	Softcover
1-4218-0950-8	The Turn of the Screw	James, Henry	$26.95	Hardcover
1-4218-0195-7	The Two Wives	Arthur, T. S.	$11.95	Softcover
1-59540-545-3	The U.P. Trail	Grey, Zane	$20.95	Softcover
1-4218-0895-1	The U.P. Trail	Grey, Zane	$37.95	Hardcover
1-59540-678-6	The Underdogs	Azuela, Mariano	$11.95	Softcover
1-4218-0187-6	The Unspeakable Perk	Adams, Samuel Hopkins	$12.95	Softcover
1-59540-120-2	The Upanishads	Parmananda, Swami	$10.95	Softcover
1-59540-003-6	The Valet's Tragedy	Lang, Andrew	$14.95	Softcover
1-4218-0134-5	The Valiant Runaways	Atherton, Gertrude	$11.95	Softcover
1-59540-416-3	The Valley Of Fear	Doyle, Arthur Conan	$12.95	Softcover
1-4218-0816-1	The Valley Of Fear	Doyle, Arthur Conan	$27.95	Hardcover
1-4218-1521-4	The Vanished Messenger	Oppenheim, E. Phillips	$15.95	Softcover
1-4218-0107-8	The Violet Fairy Book	Lang, Andrew	$17.95	Softcover
1-59540-417-1	The Vital Message	Doyle, Arthur Conan	$10.95	Softcover

ISBN	TITLE	AUTHOR	RETAIL	EDITION
1-59540-531-3	The Voyage Out	Woolf, Virginia	$20.95	Softcover
1-4218-0148-5	The Voyages of Doctor Dolittle	Lofting, Hugh	$14.95	Softcover
1-59540-306-X	The Wagner Story Book	Frost, Henry	$11.95	Softcover
1-59540-030-3	The War of the Worlds	Wells, H. G.	$12.95	Softcover
1-4218-0630-4	The War of the Worlds	Wells, H. G.	$27.95	Hardcover
1-4218-0153-1	The Way of Peace	Allen, James	$10.95	Softcover
1-4218-1129-4	The Ways of Men	Gregory, Eliot	$13.95	Softcover
1-59540-524-0	The Well Beloved	Hardy, Thomas	$13.95	Softcover
1-4218-0425-5	The Were-Wolf	Housman, Clemence	$10.95	Softcover
1-59540-418-X	The White Company	Doyle, Arthur Conan	$21.95	Softcover
1-4218-0127-2	The White Moll	Packard, Frank L.	$14.95	Softcover
1-59540-004-4	The Wife	Chekhov, Anton	$14.95	Softcover
1-4218-0604-5	The Wife	Chekhov, Anton	$29.95	Hardcover
1-59540-046-X	The Wind in the Willows	Grahame, Kenneth	$12.95	Softcover
1-4218-0646-0	The Wind in the Willows	Grahame, Kenneth	$27.95	Hardcover
1-59540-005-2	The Witch	Chekhov, Anton	$14.95	Softcover
1-4218-0605-3	The Witch	Chekhov, Anton	$29.95	Hardcover
1-4218-0137-X	The Woman Who Did	Allen, Grant	$11.95	Softcover
1-4218-0037-3	The Woman Who Did	Allen, Grant	$26.95	Hardcover
1-59540-102-4	The Wonderful Wizard Of Oz	Baum, L. Frank	$11.95	Softcover
1-4218-0652-5	The Wonderful Wizard Of Oz	Baum, L. Frank	$26.95	Hardcover
1-4218-1522-2	The Yellow Crayon	Oppenheim, E. Phillips	$15.95	Softcover
1-4218-0497-2	The Yellow Streak	Williams, Valentine	$14.95	Softcover
1-4218-0432-8	The Young Captives	Jones, Erasmus W.	$12.95	Softcover
1-4218-0146-9	The Young Explorer	Alger Jr., Horatio	$12.95	Softcover
1-59540-546-1	The Young Forester	Grey, Zane	$12.95	Softcover
1-4218-0896-X	The Young Forester	Grey, Zane	$27.95	Hardcover
1-4218-1145-6	The Young Musician	Alger Jr., Horatio	$13.95	Softcover
1-4218-0151-5	The Young Woodsman	Oxley, J. Macdonald	$10.95	Softcover
1-59540-014-1	The Zeppelin's Passenger	Oppenheim, E. Phillips	$14.95	Softcover
1-4218-0190-6	This Is The End	Benson, Stella	$11.95	Softcover
1-59540-616-6	This Simian World	Day Jr., Clarence	$10.95	Softcover
1-59540-825-8	Thomas Jefferson	Ellis, Edward S.	$11.95	Softcover
1-4218-1526-5	Thomas Jefferson	Ellis, Edward S.	$11.95	Softcover
1-4218-0161-2	Three Men on the Bummel	Jerome, Jerome K.	$13.95	Softcover
1-59540-106-7	Through The Looking-Glass	Carroll, Lewis	$10.95	Softcover

ISBN	TITLE	AUTHOR	RETAIL	EDITION
1-4218-0656-8	Through The Looking-Glass	Carroll, Lewis	$26.95	Hardcover
1-59540-227-6	Thuvia, Maid Of Mars	Burroughs, Edgar Rice	$12.95	Softcover
1-4218-0727-0	Thuvia, Maid Of Mars	Burroughs, Edgar Rice	$27.95	Hardcover
1-4218-0461-1	Till the Clock Stops	Bell, John Joy	$14.95	Softcover
1-4218-1551-6	Timothy Crump's Ward	Alger Jr., Horatio	$12.95	Softcover
1-59540-547-X	To The Last Man	Grey, Zane	$15.95	Softcover
1-4218-0897-8	To The Last Man	Grey, Zane	$31.95	Hardcover
1-59540-329-9	Tom Sawyer Abroad	Twain, Mark	$10.95	Softcover
1-59540-330-2	Tom Sawyer Detective	Twain, Mark	$10.95	Softcover
1-4218-1186-3	Tom Swift Among the Diamond Makers	Appleton, Victor	$11.95	Softcover
1-4218-1188-X	Tom Swift Among the Fire Fighters	Appleton, Victor	$12.95	Softcover
1-4218-1192-8	Tom Swift and His Aerial Warship	Appleton, Victor	$12.95	Softcover
1-4218-1191-X	Tom Swift and His Air Scout	Appleton, Victor	$12.95	Softcover
1-59540-806-1	Tom Swift and His Airship	Appleton, Victor	$12.95	Softcover
1-4218-1193-6	Tom Swift and His Big Tunnel	Appleton, Victor	$12.95	Softcover
1-4218-1187-1	Tom Swift and His Electric Locomotive	Appleton, Victor	$12.95	Softcover
1-59540-807-X	Tom Swift and His Electric Rifle	Appleton, Victor	$11.95	Softcover
1-4218-1189-8	Tom Swift and His Giant Cannon	Appleton, Victor	$12.95	Softcover
1-4218-1190-1	Tom Swift and his Great Searchlight	Appleton, Victor	$12.95	Softcover
1-4218-1600-8	Tom Swift and his Motor-Boat	Appleton, Victor	$11.95	Softcover
1-4218-1601-6	Tom Swift and his Motor-Boat	Appleton, Victor	$11.95	Softcover
1-4218-1602-4	Tom Swift and his Motor-Cycle	Appleton, Victor	$11.95	Softcover
1-4218-1603-2	Tom Swift and his Photo Telephone	Appleton, Victor	$12.95	Softcover
1-4218-1604-0	Tom Swift and his Sky Racer	Appleton, Victor	$11.95	Softcover
1-4218-1605-9	Tom Swift and his War Tank	Appleton, Victor	$12.95	Softcover
1-4218-1606-7	Tom Swift and his Wireless Message	Appleton, Victor	$11.95	Softcover
1-4218-1607-5	Tom Swift and his Wizard Camera	Appleton, Victor	$11.95	Softcover
1-4218-1608-3	Tom Swift in Captivity	Appleton, Victor	$12.95	Softcover
1-4218-1609-1	Tom Swift in the Caves of Ice	Appleton, Victor	$12.95	Softcover
1-4218-1610-5	Tom Swift in the City of Gold	Appleton, Victor	$12.95	Softcover
1-4218-1611-3	Tom Swift in the Land of Wonders	Appleton, Victor	$12.95	Softcover

ISBN	TITLE	AUTHOR	RETAIL	EDITION
1-59540-515-1	Treasure Island	Stevenson, R. L.	$13.95	Softcover
1-4218-0865-X	Treasure Island	Stevenson, R. L.	$28.95	Hardcover
1-59540-680-8	Trials and Triumphs of Faith	Cole, Mary	$13.95	Softcover
1-4218-0487-5	Triumph of the Egg	Anderson, Sherwood	$12.95	Softcover
1-4218-1559-1	Try and Trust	Alger Jr., Horatio	$13.95	Softcover
1-59540-044-3	Twenty Thousand Leagues Under The Sea	Verne, Jules	$17.95	Softcover
1-4218-0644-4	Twenty Thousand Leagues Under The Sea	Verne, Jules	$33.95	Hardcover
1-59540-525-9	Two On A Tower	Hardy, Thomas	$17.95	Softcover
1-59540-121-0	Two Years in the Forbidden City	Der Ling, The Princess	$14.95	Softcover
1-4218-0671-1	Two Years in the Forbidden City	Der Ling, The Princess	$29.95	Hardcover
1-59540-656-5	Umboo, The Elephant	Garis, Howard R.	$10.95	Softcover
1-59540-031-1	Uncle Tom's Cabin	Stowe, Harriet Beecher	$26.95	Softcover
1-4218-0631-2	Uncle Tom's Cabin	Stowe, Harriet Beecher	$45.95	Hardcover
1-59540-205-5	Uncle Vanya	Chekhov, Anton	$10.95	Softcover
1-4218-1568-0	Uncle Wiggily's Adventures	Garis, Howard R.	$11.95	Softcover
1-4218-1569-9	Uncle Wiggily's Travels	Garis, Howard R.	$11.95	Softcover
1-4218-1587-7	Under The Lilacs	Alcott, Louisa May	$13.95	Softcover
1-4218-0489-1	Under the Red Robe	Weyman, Stanley	$13.95	Softcover
1-59540-123-7	Utopia	More, Thomas	$10.95	Softcover
1-4218-0673-8	Utopia	More, Thomas	$26.95	Hardcover
1-4218-0191-4	Vedanta Philosophy	Abhedananda, Swami	$10.95	Softcover
1-59540-032-X	Walden	Thoreau, Henry David	$15.95	Softcover
1-4218-0632-0	Walden	Thoreau, Henry David	$31.95	Hardcover
1-59540-033-8	Walking	Thoreau, Henry David	$10.95	Softcover
1-4218-1560-5	Walter Sherwood's Probation	Alger Jr., Horatio	$13.95	Softcover
1-59540-232-2	Warlord Of Mars	Burroughs, Edgar Rice	$12.95	Softcover
1-4218-0732-7	Warlord Of Mars	Burroughs, Edgar Rice	$27.95	Hardcover
1-4218-1104-9	Wells Brothers	Adams, Andy	$12.95	Softcover
1-59540-331-0	What Is Man	Twain, Mark	$15.95	Softcover
1-4218-0781-5	What Is Man	Twain, Mark	$31.95	Hardcover
1-4218-1141-3	What's Wrong With The World	Cherston, G.K.	$12.95	Softcover
1-59540-637-9	When The Sleeper Wakes	Wells, H. G.	$14.95	Softcover
1-4218-0937-0	When The Sleeper Wakes	Wells, H. G.	$29.95	Hardcover

ISBN	TITLE	AUTHOR	RETAIL	EDITION
1-4218-1572-9	White Fang	London, Jack	$13.95	Softcover
1-59540-548-8	Wildfire	Grey, Zane	$17.95	Softcover
1-4218-0898-6	Wildfire	Grey, Zane	$33.95	Hardcover
1-4218-0100-0	With The Turks in Palestine	Aaronsohn, Alexander	$10.95	Softcover
1-59540-669-7	Within the Tides	Conrad, Joseph	$12.95	Softcover
1-4218-0474-3	Yet Again	Beerbohm, Max	$12.95	Softcover
1-59540-304-3	You Never Can Tell	Shaw, George Bernard	$11.95	Softcover
1-4218-0754-8	You Never Can Tell	Shaw, George Bernard	$26.95	Hardcover

TITLES BY AUTHOR

ISBN	TITLE	AUTHOR	RETAIL	EDITION
1-4218-0100-0	With The Turks in Palestine	Aaronsohn, Alexander	$10.95	Softcover
1-4218-0152-3	History of King Charles The Second of England	Abbot, Jacob	$12.95	Softcover
1-4218-0164-7	Seven Wives and Seven Prisons	Abbot, L. A.	$10.95	Softcover
1-4218-0459-X	Cleopatra	Abbott, Jacob	$12.95	Softcover
1-4218-0191-4	Vedanta Philosophy	Abhedananda, Swami	$10.95	Softcover
1-4218-0150-7	Judaism	Abrahams, Israel	$10.95	Softcover
1-4218-0192-2	The Story of Creation	Ackland, T. S.	$11.95	Softcover
1-4218-1105-7	A Texas Matchmaker	Adams, Andy	$13.95	Softcover
1-4218-1106-5	The Outlet	Adams, Andy	$13.95	Softcover
1-4218-1104-9	Wells Brothers	Adams, Andy	$12.95	Softcover
1-4218-0451-4	Democracy An American Novel	Adams, Henry	$13.95	Softcover
1-4218-0177-9	Small Means And Great Ends	Adams, M. H.	$10.95	Softcover
1-4218-1185-5	Average Jones	Adams, Samuel Hopkins	$13.95	Softcover
1-4218-1596-6	From A Bench in our Square	Adams, Samuel Hopkins	$14.95	Softcover
1-4218-0187-6	The Unspeakable Perk	Adams, Samuel Hopkins	$12.95	Softcover
1-4218-0129-9	The Slim Princess	Ade, George	$10.95	Softcover
1-59540-600-X	Aesop's Fables	Aesop	$11.95	Softcover
1-59540-676-X	Eight Cousins	Alcott, Louisa May	$14.95	Softcover
1-4218-1169-3	Jack and Jill	Alcott, Louisa May	$14.95	Softcover
1-4218-1583-4	A Garland for Girls	Alcott, Louisa May	$12.95	Softcover
1-4218-1584-2	An Old Fashioned Girl	Alcott, Louisa May	$14.95	Softcover
1-59540-107-5	Flower Fables	Alcott, Louisa May	$10.95	Softcover
1-4218-0657-6	Flower Fables	Alcott, Louisa May	$26.95	Hardcover
1-59540-108-3	Hospital Sketches	Alcott, Louisa May	$10.95	Softcover
1-4218-0658-4	Hospital Sketches	Alcott, Louisa May	$26.95	Hardcover

ISBN	TITLE	AUTHOR	RETAIL	EDITION
1-4218-1585-0	Kitty's Class Day and Other Stories	Alcott, Louisa May	$13.95	Softcover
1-4218-1586-9	Rose in Bloom	Alcott, Louisa May	$14.95	Softcover
1-4218-1587-7	Under The Lilacs	Alcott, Louisa May	$13.95	Softcover
1-4218-1598-2	The Queen of Sheba & My Cousin the Colonel	Aldrich, Thomad Bailey	$12.95	Softcover
1-4218-0495-6	The Stillwater Tragedy	Aldrich, Thomas Bailey	$13.95	Softcover
1-4218-0198-1	An Old Town By The Sea	Aldrich, Thomas Bailey	$10.95	Softcover
1-4218-0199-X	The Story Of A Bad Boy	Aldrich, Thomas Bailey	$12.95	Softcover
1-4218-0099-3	The Story Of A Bad Boy	Aldrich, Thomas Bailey	$27.95	Hardcover
1-4218-0141-8	Bound To Rise	Alger Jr., Horatio	$13.95	Softcover
1-4218-0041-1	Bound To Rise	Alger Jr., Horatio	$28.95	Hardcover
1-4218-1552-4	Brave and Bold	Alger Jr., Horatio	$13.95	Softcover
1-4218-1553-2	Driven From Home	Alger Jr., Horatio	$14.95	Softcover
1-4218-0142-6	Facing The World	Alger Jr., Horatio	$11.95	Softcover
1-4218-0143-4	Helping Himself	Alger Jr., Horatio	$13.95	Softcover
1-4218-1554-0	Jack's Ward	Alger Jr., Horatio	$13.95	Softcover
1-4218-0144-2	Joe The Hotel Boy	Alger Jr., Horatio	$12.95	Softcover
1-4218-1555-9	Joe's Luck	Alger Jr., Horatio	$13.95	Softcover
1-4218-1556-7	Making His Way	Alger Jr., Horatio	$13.95	Softcover
1-4218-1557-5	Ragged Dick	Alger Jr., Horatio	$12.95	Softcover
1-4218-1558-3	Risen From the Ranks	Alger Jr., Horatio	$13.95	Softcover
1-4218-0145-0	The Cash Boy	Alger Jr., Horatio	$11.95	Softcover
1-4218-0455-7	The Errand Boy	Alger Jr., Horatio	$14.95	Softcover
1-59540-654-9	The Store Boy	Alger Jr., Horatio	$13.95	Softcover
1-4218-0954-0	The Store Boy	Alger Jr., Horatio	$28.95	Hardcover
1-4218-0146-9	The Young Explorer	Alger Jr., Horatio	$12.95	Softcover
1-4218-1145-6	The Young Musician	Alger Jr., Horatio	$13.95	Softcover
1-4218-1551-6	Timothy Crump's Ward	Alger Jr., Horatio	$12.95	Softcover
1-4218-1559-1	Try and Trust	Alger Jr., Horatio	$13.95	Softcover
1-4218-1560-5	Walter Sherwood's Probation	Alger Jr., Horatio	$13.95	Softcover
1-59540-634-4	An African Millionaire	Allen, Grant	$13.95	Softcover
1-4218-1544-3	Hilda Wade	Allen, Grant	$13.95	Softcover
1-4218-1545-1	Michael's Crag	Allen, Grant	$10.95	Softcover
1-4218-0135-3	Recalled To Life	Allen, Grant	$12.95	Softcover
1-4218-0136-1	The British Barbarians	Allen, Grant	$10.95	Softcover

ISBN	TITLE	AUTHOR	RETAIL	EDITION
1-4218-1546-X	The Great Taboo	Allen, Grant	$13.95	Softcover
1-4218-0137-X	The Woman Who Did	Allen, Grant	$11.95	Softcover
1-4218-0037-3	The Woman Who Did	Allen, Grant	$26.95	Hardcover
1-4218-0153-1	The Way of Peace	Allen, James	$10.95	Softcover
1-4218-0156-6	The Bride of The Mistletoe	Allen, James Lane	$10.95	Softcover
1-4218-0460-3	The Choir Invisible	Allen, James Lane	$13.95	Softcover
1-4218-1573-7	The Reign of Law	Allen, James Lane	$13.95	Softcover
1-4218-0186-8	An American Robinson Crusoe	Allison, Samuel B.	$10.95	Softcover
1-59540-809-6	The Delicious Vice	Allison, Young E.	$10.95	Softcover
1-4218-1154-5	The Scouts of the Valley	Altsheler, Joseph A.	$14.95	Softcover
1-4218-1577-X	The Free Rangers	Altsheler, Joseph A.	$14.95	Softcover
1-4218-0180-9	Free From School	Alvares, Rahul	$10.95	Softcover
1-59540-305-1	Andersen's Fairy Tales	Andersen, Hans Christian	$12.95	Softcover
1-4218-0755-6	Andersen's Fairy Tales	Andersen, Hans Christian	$27.95	Hardcover
1-4218-0182-5	Half Past Seven Stories	Anderson, Robert Gordon	$12.95	Softcover
1-4218-0183-3	Seven O'Clock Stories	Anderson, Robert Gordon	$11.95	Softcover
1-4218-0488-3	Marching Men	Anderson, Sherwood	$13.95	Softcover
1-4218-1597-4	Poor White	Anderson, Sherwood	$15.95	Softcover
1-4218-0487-5	Triumph of the Egg	Anderson, Sherwood	$12.95	Softcover
1-4218-0197-3	A Tale of One City	Anderton, Thomas	$10.95	Softcover
1-4218-0154-X	The Stories Mother Nature Told Her Children	Andrews, James	$10.95	Softcover
1-4218-1168-5	The Crushed Flower and Other Stories	Andreyev, Leonid	$14.95	Softcover
1-4218-0168-X	The Seven Who Were Hanged	Andreyev, Leonid	$10.95	Softcover
1-4218-0178-7	The Firefly of France	Angellotti, Marion Polk	$13.95	Softcover
1-59540-000-1	Cinderella	Anonymous	$10.95	Softcover
1-4218-0600-2	Cinderella	Anonymous	$26.95	Hardcover
1-4218-1186-3	Tom Swift Among the Diamond Makers	Appleton, Victor	$11.95	Softcover
1-4218-1188-X	Tom Swift Among the Fire Fighters	Appleton, Victor	$12.95	Softcover
1-4218-1192-8	Tom Swift and His Aerial Warship	Appleton, Victor	$12.95	Softcover
1-4218-1191-X	Tom Swift and His Air Scout	Appleton, Victor	$12.95	Softcover
1-4218-1193-6	Tom Swift and His Big Tunnel	Appleton, Victor	$12.95	Softcover
1-4218-1187-1	Tom Swift and His Electric	Appleton, Victor	$12.95	Softcover

ISBN	TITLE	AUTHOR	RETAIL	EDITION
1-4218-1189-8	Tom Swift and His Giant Locomotive Cannon	Appleton, Victor	$12.95	Softcover
1-4218-1190-1	Tom Swift and his Great Searchlight	Appleton, Victor	$12.95	Softcover
1-4218-1599-0	The Moving Picture Boys at Panama	Appleton, Victor	$12.95	Softcover
1-59540-806-1	Tom Swift and His Airship	Appleton, Victor	$12.95	Softcover
1-59540-807-X	Tom Swift and His Electric Rifle	Appleton, Victor	$11.95	Softcover
1-4218-1600-8	Tom Swift and his Motor-Boat	Appleton, Victor	$11.95	Softcover
1-4218-1601-6	Tom Swift and his Motor-Boat	Appleton, Victor	$11.95	Softcover
1-4218-1602-4	Tom Swift and his Motor-Cycle	Appleton, Victor	$11.95	Softcover
1-4218-1603-2	Tom Swift and his Photo Telephone	Appleton, Victor	$12.95	Softcover
1-4218-1604-0	Tom Swift and his Sky Racer	Appleton, Victor	$11.95	Softcover
1-4218-1605-9	Tom Swift and his War Tank	Appleton, Victor	$12.95	Softcover
1-4218-1606-7	Tom Swift and his Wireless Message	Appleton, Victor	$11.95	Softcover
1-4218-1607-5	Tom Swift and his Wizard Camera	Appleton, Victor	$11.95	Softcover
1-4218-1608-3	Tom Swift in Captivity	Appleton, Victor	$12.95	Softcover
1-4218-1609-1	Tom Swift in the Caves of Ice	Appleton, Victor	$12.95	Softcover
1-4218-1610-5	Tom Swift in the City of Gold	Appleton, Victor	$12.95	Softcover
1-4218-1611-3	Tom Swift in the Land of Wonders	Appleton, Victor	$12.95	Softcover
1-4218-0431-X	Gulliver of Mars	Arnold, Edwin L.	$13.95	Softcover
1-4218-0193-0	After A Shadow	Arthur, T. S.	$11.95	Softcover
1-4218-0194-9	After The Storm	Arthur, T. S.	$13.95	Softcover
1-4218-0494-8	The Allen House	Arthur, T. S.	$14.95	Softcover
1-4218-0195-7	The Two Wives	Arthur, T. S.	$11.95	Softcover
1-4218-0133-7	Sleeping Fires	Atherton, Gertrude	$12.95	Softcover
1-4218-0134-5	The Valiant Runaways	Atherton, Gertrude	$11.95	Softcover
1-4218-0123-X	Greyfriars Bobby	Atkins, Eleanor	$12.95	Softcover
1-4218-0023-3	Greyfriars Bobby	Atkins, Eleanor	$27.95	Hardcover
1-59540-610-7	Our Churches and Chapels	Atticus	$15.95	Softcover
1-59540-438-4	Emma	Austen, Jane	$22.95	Softcover
1-59540-037-0	Mansfield Park	Austen, Jane	$21.95	Softcover
1-4218-0637-1	Mansfield Park	Austen, Jane	$39.95	Hardcover
1-59540-038-9	Persuasion	Austen, Jane	$14.95	Softcover
1-4218-0638-X	Persuasion	Austen, Jane	$29.95	Hardcover

ISBN	TITLE	AUTHOR	RETAIL	EDITION
1-59540-440-6	Pride and prejudice	Austen, Jane	$18.95	Softcover
1-4218-0840-4	Pride and prejudice	Austen, Jane	$35.95	Hardcover
1-59540-439-2	Sense and Sensibility	Austen, Jane	$17.95	Softcover
1-4218-0839-0	Sense and Sensibility	Austen, Jane	$33.95	Hardcover
1-4218-0160-4	Northanger Abbey	Austen, Jane	$14.95	Softcover
1-59540-436-8	Outpost	Austin, J. G.	$14.95	Softcover
1-59540-679-4	The Land of Little Rain	Austin, Mary	$10.95	Softcover
1-4218-0979-6	The Land of Little Rain	Austin, Mary	$26.95	Hardcover
1-59540-642-5	The Triple Alliance	Avery, Harold	$14.95	Softcover
1-59540-678-6	The Underdogs	Azuela, Mariano	$11.95	Softcover
1-4218-1147-2	The Master of Silence	Bacheller, Irving	$10.95	Softcover
1-59540-233-0	Essays of Francis Bacon	Bacon, Francis	$12.95	Softcover
1-4218-0733-5	Essays of Francis Bacon	Bacon, Francis	$27.95	Hardcover
1-4218-1112-X	Creation and Its Records	Baden-Powell, B. H.	$12.95	Softcover
1-4218-1155-3	The Lost City	Badger Jr., Joseph E.	$12.95	Softcover
1-4218-1133-2	The Happy Foreigner	Bagnold, Enid	$12.95	Softcover
1-4218-1142-1	The Highwayman	Bailey, H.C.	$14.95	Softcover
1-59540-808-8	The Boy Ranchers on the Trail	Baker, Willard F.	$12.95	Softcover
1-4218-1152-9	The Story of Siegfried	Baldwin, James	$13.95	Softcover
1-4218-0155-8	Old Greek Stories	Baldwin, James	$11.95	Softcover
1-4218-1593-1	Great Astronomers	Ball, R. S.	$13.95	Softcover
1-4218-0485-9	Martin Rattler	Ballantyne, Robert Michael	$12.95	Softcover
1-59540-653-0	The Deserted Woman	Balzac, Honore De	$10.95	Softcover
1-4218-0453-0	The Girl with the Golden Eyes	Balzac, Honore de	$10.95	Softcover
1-4218-1153-7	A Rebellious Heroine	Bangs, John Kendrick	$10.95	Softcover
1-4218-1574-5	The Enchanted Typewriter	Bangs, John Kendrick	$10.95	Softcover
1-4218-1575-3	The Pursuit of the House-Boat	Bangs, John Kendrick	$10.95	Softcover
1-4218-1176-6	The Adventure Club Afloat	Barbour, Ralph Henry	$12.95	Softcover
1-4218-1594-X	The Half-Back	Barbour, Ralph Henry	$12.95	Softcover
1-4218-1595-8	The Lilac Girl	Barbour, Ralph Henry	$10.95	Softcover
1-4218-1547-8	The Inferno	Barbusse, Henri	$11.95	Softcover
1-4218-0403-4	A Knight of the Nets	Barr, Amelia E.	$13.95	Softcover
1-4218-0181-7	One Days Courtship and the Heralds of Fame	Barr, Robert	$11.95	Softcover
1-59540-036-2	The Adventures of Peter Pan	Barrie, J. M.	$12.95	Softcover
1-4218-0636-3	The Adventures of Peter Pan	Barrie, J. M.	$27.95	Hardcover

ISBN	TITLE	AUTHOR	RETAIL	EDITION
1-59540-672-7	American Fairy Tales	Baum, L. Frank	$10.95	Softcover
1-4218-0464-6	The Emerald City of Oz	Baum, L. Frank	$13.95	Softcover
1-4218-1580-X	The Enchanted Island of Yew	Baum, L. Frank	$11.95	Softcover
1-4218-1531-1	The Life and Adventures of Santa Clause	Baum, L. Frank	$10.95	Softcover
1-59540-047-8	The Lost Princess of Oz	Baum, L. Frank	$12.95	Softcover
1-4218-0647-9	The Lost Princess of Oz	Baum, L. Frank	$27.95	Hardcover
1-59540-101-6	The Magic of Oz	Baum, L. Frank	$11.95	Softcover
1-4218-0651-7	The Magic of Oz	Baum, L. Frank	$26.95	Hardcover
1-59540-100-8	The Marvelous Land of Oz	Baum, L. Frank	$12.95	Softcover
1-4218-0650-9	The Marvelous Land of Oz	Baum, L. Frank	$27.95	Hardcover
1-4218-0165-5	The Road to Oz	Baum, L. Frank	$11.95	Softcover
1-59540-102-4	The Wonderful Wizard Of Oz	Baum, L. Frank	$11.95	Softcover
1-4218-0652-5	The Wonderful Wizard Of Oz	Baum, L. Frank	$26.95	Hardcover
1-4218-1177-4	The Barrier	Beach, Rex	$14.95	Softcover
1-4218-0482-4	Pardners	Beach, Rex E.	$11.95	Softcover
1-4218-0474-3	Yet Again	Beerbohm, Max	$12.95	Softcover
1-59540-149-0	Beethoven: The Man and the Artist	Beethoven, Ludwig van	$10.95	Softcover
1-4218-0699-1	Beethoven: The Man and the Artist	Beethoven, Ludwig van	$26.95	Hardcover
1-4218-0461-1	Till the Clock Stops	Bell, John Joy	$14.95	Softcover
1-4218-0169-8	From A Girls Point Of View	Bell, Lilian	$10.95	Softcover
1-4218-0404-2	The Grand Babylon Hotel	Bennett, Arnold	$14.95	Softcover
1-4218-0190-6	This Is The End	Benson, Stella	$11.95	Softcover
1-4218-0486-7	The Idol of Paris	Bernhardt, Sarah	$14.95	Softcover
1-59540-200-4	An Introduction To Yoga	Besant, Annie	$10.95	Softcover
1-4218-0402-6	Present at a Hanging	Bierce, Ambrose	$10.95	Softcover
1-4218-1516-8	A Happy Boy	Bjornson, Bjornstjerne	$10.95	Softcover
1-4218-1157-X	How It Happened	Bosher, Kate Langley	$10.95	Softcover
1-4218-0463-8	The Man in Lonely Land	Bosher, Kate Langley	$11.95	Softcover
1-4218-1111-1	Cabin Fever	Bower, B. M.	$11.95	Softcover
1-4218-1514-1	Casey Ryan	Bower, B. M.	$12.95	Softcover
1-4218-0405-0	The Phantom Herd	Bower, B. M.	$13.95	Softcover
1-4218-1110-3	The Range Dwellers	Bower, B. M.	$10.95	Softcover
1-4218-1515-X	The Thunder Bird	Bower, B. M.	$13.95	Softcover
1-4218-1114-6	The Happy Family	Bower, Bertha Muzzy	$12.95	Softcover
1-4218-1173-1	The Fortieth Door	Bradley, Mary Hastings	$13.95	Softcover

ISBN	TITLE	AUTHOR	RETAIL	EDITION
1-4218-0416-6	Coralie	Braeme, Charlotte M.	$10.95	Softcover
1-4218-1175-8	The Light That Lures	Brebner, Percy	$14.95	Softcover
1-59540-011-7	The Complete Works Of Artemus Ward, Part 3	Browne, Charles Farrar	$10.95	Softcover
1-59540-805-3	Legends of Charlemagne	Bulfinch, Thomas	$17.95	Softcover
1-4218-0496-4	Happy Jack	Burgess, Thornton W.	$10.95	Softcover
1-59540-695-6	The Adventures of Reddy Fox	Burgess, Thornton W.	$10.95	Softcover
1-59540-696-4	The Burgess Animal Book for Children	Burgess, Thornton W.	$14.95	Softcover
1-4218-0427-1	The Hilltop Boys on the River	Burleigh, Cyril	$11.95	Softcover
1-59540-019-2	The Secret Garden	Burnett, Frances Hodgson	$14.95	Softcover
1-4218-0619-3	The Secret Garden	Burnett, Frances Hodgson	$29.95	Hardcover
1-59540-208-X	At The Earths Core	Burroughs, Edgar Rice	$11.95	Softcover
1-4218-0708-4	At The Earths Core	Burroughs, Edgar Rice	$26.95	Hardcover
1-59540-209-8	Gods Of Mars	Burroughs, Edgar Rice	$14.95	Softcover
1-4218-0709-2	Gods Of Mars	Burroughs, Edgar Rice	$29.95	Hardcover
1-59540-228-4	Out Of Times Abyss	Burroughs, Edgar Rice	$10.95	Softcover
1-59540-229-2	Pellucidar	Burroughs, Edgar Rice	$12.95	Softcover
1-59540-230-6	People Out Of Time	Burroughs, Edgar Rice	$10.95	Softcover
1-4218-0730-0	People Out Of Time	Burroughs, Edgar Rice	$26.95	Hardcover
1-59540-231-4	Princess Of Mars	Burroughs, Edgar Rice	$13.95	Softcover
1-59540-210-1	Tarzan And The Jewels of Opar	Burroughs, Edgar Rice	$13.95	Softcover
1-4218-0710-6	Tarzan And The Jewels of Opar	Burroughs, Edgar Rice	$28.95	Hardcover
1-59540-211-X	Tarzan of the Apes	Burroughs, Edgar Rice	$15.95	Softcover
1-4218-0711-4	Tarzan of the Apes	Burroughs, Edgar Rice	$31.95	Hardcover
1-59540-212-8	Tarzan the Terrible	Burroughs, Edgar Rice	$15.95	Softcover
1-4218-0712-2	Tarzan the Terrible	Burroughs, Edgar Rice	$31.95	Hardcover
1-59540-213-6	Tarzan the Untamed	Burroughs, Edgar Rice	$17.95	Softcover
1-4218-0713-0	Tarzan the Untamed	Burroughs, Edgar Rice	$33.95	Hardcover
1-59540-214-4	The Beasts Of Tarzan	Burroughs, Edgar Rice	$13.95	Softcover
1-4218-0714-9	The Beasts Of Tarzan	Burroughs, Edgar Rice	$28.95	Hardcover
1-59540-215-2	The Chessmen of Mars	Burroughs, Edgar Rice	$14.95	Softcover
1-4218-0715-7	The Chessmen of Mars	Burroughs, Edgar Rice	$29.95	Hardcover
1-59540-216-0	The Efficiency Expert	Burroughs, Edgar Rice	$12.95	Softcover
1-4218-0716-5	The Efficiency Expert	Burroughs, Edgar Rice	$27.95	Hardcover
1-59540-217-9	The Jungle Tales Of Tarzan	Burroughs, Edgar Rice	$13.95	Softcover

ISBN	TITLE	AUTHOR	RETAIL	EDITION
1-4218-0717-3	The Jungle Tales Of Tarzan	Burroughs, Edgar Rice	$28.95	Hardcover
1-59540-218-7	The Land that Time Forgot	Burroughs, Edgar Rice	$10.95	Softcover
1-59540-219-5	The Lost Continent	Burroughs, Edgar Rice	$11.95	Softcover
1-59540-220-9	The Mad King	Burroughs, Edgar Rice	$15.95	Softcover
1-59540-221-7	The Monster Men	Burroughs, Edgar Rice	$12.95	Softcover
1-59540-222-5	The Mucker	Burroughs, Edgar Rice	$20.95	Softcover
1-59540-223-3	The Oakdale Affair	Burroughs, Edgar Rice	$11.95	Softcover
1-59540-224-1	The Outlaw of Torn	Burroughs, Edgar Rice	$13.95	Softcover
1-59540-225-X	The Return Of Tarzan	Burroughs, Edgar Rice	$15.95	Softcover
1-59540-226-8	The Son Of Tarzan	Burroughs, Edgar Rice	$15.95	Softcover
1-4218-0726-2	The Son Of Tarzan	Burroughs, Edgar Rice	$31.95	Hardcover
1-59540-227-6	Thuvia, Maid Of Mars	Burroughs, Edgar Rice	$12.95	Softcover
1-4218-0727-0	Thuvia, Maid Of Mars	Burroughs, Edgar Rice	$27.95	Hardcover
1-59540-232-2	Warlord Of Mars	Burroughs, Edgar Rice	$12.95	Softcover
1-4218-0732-7	Warlord Of Mars	Burroughs, Edgar Rice	$27.95	Hardcover
1-59540-041-9	Birds and Poets	Burroughs, John	$12.95	Softcover
1-4218-1116-2	Action Front	Cable, Boyd	$12.95	Softcover
1-59540-633-6	Strong Hearts	Cable, George W.	$12.95	Softcover
1-4218-1543-5	The Cavalier	Cable, George W.	$14.95	Softcover
1-59540-608-5	The Freedom of Life	Call, Annie Payson	$10.95	Softcover
1-4218-1194-4	Keeping Fit All the Way	Camp, Walter	$10.95	Softcover
1-4218-0462-X	By The Golden Gate	Carey, Joseph	$11.95	Softcover
1-59540-689-1	Esther	Carey, Rosa Nouchette	$14.95	Softcover
1-59540-442-2	Alice's Adventure In Wonderland	Carroll, Lewis	$10.95	Softcover
1-4218-0842-0	Alice's Adventure In Wonderland	Carroll, Lewis	$26.95	Hardcover
1-59540-443-0	Sylvie And Bruno	Carroll, Lewis	$14.95	Softcover
1-4218-0843-9	Sylvie And Bruno	Carroll, Lewis	$29.95	Hardcover
1-59540-106-7	Through The Looking-Glass	Carroll, Lewis	$10.95	Softcover
1-4218-0656-8	Through The Looking-Glass	Carroll, Lewis	$26.95	Hardcover
1-59540-652-2	The History of The Telephone	Casson, Herbert N.	$11.95	Softcover
1-59540-698-0	Alexander's Bridge	Cather, Willa	$10.95	Softcover
1-4218-0185-X	In the Quarter	Chambers, Robert W.	$13.95	Softcover
1-4218-1107-3	The Bishop and Other Stories	Chekhov, Anton	$13.95	Softcover
1-4218-1108-1	The Duel and Other Stories	Chekhov, Anton	$13.95	Softcover
1-59540-201-2	Ivanoff	Chekhov, Anton	$10.95	Softcover

ISBN	TITLE	AUTHOR	RETAIL	EDITION
1-59540-202-0	The Letters of Anton Chekhov	Chekhov, Anton	$20.95	Softcover
1-4218-0702-5	The Letters of Anton Chekhov	Chekhov, Anton	$37.95	Hardcover
1-59540-203-9	The School Mistress	Chekhov, Anton	$13.95	Softcover
1-59540-204-7	The Sea-Gull	Chekhov, Anton	$10.95	Softcover
1-59540-004-4	The Wife	Chekhov, Anton	$14.95	Softcover
1-4218-0604-5	The Wife	Chekhov, Anton	$29.95	Hardcover
1-59540-005-2	The Witch	Chekhov, Anton	$14.95	Softcover
1-4218-0605-3	The Witch	Chekhov, Anton	$29.95	Hardcover
1-59540-205-5	Uncle Vanya	Chekhov, Anton	$10.95	Softcover
1-4218-1134-0	Buffalo Roost	Cheley, F.H.	$12.95	Softcover
1-4218-1139-1	The New Jerusalem	Cherston, G.K.	$13.95	Softcover
1-4218-1141-3	What's Wrong With The World	Cherston, G.K.	$12.95	Softcover
1-4218-1103-0	The Secret Adversary	Christie, Agatha	$15.95	Softcover
1-59540-601-8	The Mysterious Affair at Styles	Christie, Agatha	$13.95	Softcover
1-59540-128-8	A Far Country, Vol1	Churchill, Winston	$12.95	Softcover
1-59540-129-6	A Far Country, Vol2	Churchill, Winston	$12.95	Softcover
1-59540-130-X	A Traveller In War Time	Churchill, Winston	$10.95	Softcover
1-59540-131-8	Dr. Jonathan	Churchill, Winston	$10.95	Softcover
1-59540-132-6	Mr. Crewes Career	Churchill, Winston	$24.95	Softcover
1-59540-133-4	On The American Contribution	Churchill, Winston	$10.95	Softcover
1-59540-134-2	The Celebrity	Churchill, Winston	$12.95	Softcover
1-59540-135-0	The Crisis	Churchill, Winston	$26.95	Softcover
1-4218-0685-1	The Crisis	Churchill, Winston	$45.95	Hardcover
1-59540-136-9	The Dwelling-Place of Light, Vol 1	Churchill, Winston	$11.95	Softcover
1-59540-137-7	The Dwelling-Place of Light, Vol 2	Churchill, Winston	$11.95	Softcover
1-59540-138-5	The Dwelling-Place of Light, Vol 3	Churchill, Winston	$11.95	Softcover
1-59540-139-3	The Inside of The Cup Vol 1.	Churchill, Winston	$10.95	Softcover
1-59540-140-7	The Inside of The Cup Vol 2.	Churchill, Winston	$10.95	Softcover
1-59540-141-5	The Inside of The Cup Vol 3.	Churchill, Winston	$10.95	Softcover
1-59540-142-3	The Inside of The Cup Vol 4.	Churchill, Winston	$10.95	Softcover
1-59540-143-1	The Inside of The Cup Vol 5.	Churchill, Winston	$10.95	Softcover
1-59540-144-X	The Inside of The Cup Vol 6.	Churchill, Winston	$10.95	Softcover
1-59540-145-8	The Inside of The Cup Vol 7.	Churchill, Winston	$10.95	Softcover
1-59540-146-6	The Inside of The Cup Vol 8.	Churchill, Winston	$10.95	Softcover

ISBN	TITLE	AUTHOR	RETAIL	EDITION
1-59540-624-7	The Theology of Holiness	Clark, Dougan	$10.95	Softcover
1-59540-658-1	The Man From The Clouds	Clouston, J. Storer	$13.95	Softcover
1-59540-635-2	The Fourth Watch	Cody, H. A.	$14.95	Softcover
1-59540-680-8	Trials and Triumphs of Faith	Cole, Mary	$13.95	Softcover
1-59540-697-2	The Haunted Hotel	Collins, Wilkie	$13.95	Softcover
1-4218-0997-4	The Haunted Hotel	Collins, Wilkie	$28.95	Hardcover
1-59540-008-7	The Adventures of Pinocchio	Collodi, C.	$12.95	Softcover
1-4218-0608-8	The Adventures of Pinocchio	Collodi, C.	$27.95	Hardcover
1-59540-422-8	The Analects	Confucius	$11.95	Softcover
1-59540-669-7	Within the Tides	Conrad, Joseph	$12.95	Softcover
1-4218-1143-X	The Poor Gentleman	Conscience, Hendrick	$10.95	Softcover
1-4218-1171-5	Sister Carmen	Corvus, M.	$10.95	Softcover
1-59540-630-1	The Path of A Star	Cotes, Everard	$14.95	Softcover
1-59540-692-1	Men, Women, and Boats	Crane, Stephen	$12.95	Softcover
1-59540-119-9	The Red Badge of Courage	Crane, Stephen	$11.95	Softcover
1-4218-0669-X	The Red Badge of Courage	Crane, Stephen	$26.95	Hardcover
1-59540-631-X	Beneath The Banner	Cross, F. J.	$12.95	Softcover
1-4218-1172-3	Apples, Ripe and Rosy, Sir,	Crowley, Mary Catherine	$11.95	Softcover
1-4218-0401-8	A Yankee Girl at Fort Sumter	Curtis, Alice Turner	$11.95	Softcover
1-59540-660-3	Back to God's Country	Curwood, James Oliver	$13.95	Softcover
1-4218-0960-5	Back to God's Country	Curwood, James Oliver	$28.95	Hardcover
1-59540-661-1	Baree, Son of Kazan	Curwood, James Oliver	$12.95	Softcover
1-4218-0961-3	Baree, Son of Kazan	Curwood, James Oliver	$27.95	Hardcover
1-59540-662-X	Nomads of The North	Curwood, James Oliver	$12.95	Softcover
1-4218-0962-1	Nomads of The North	Curwood, James Oliver	$27.95	Hardcover
1-4218-0157-4	The Flaming Forest	Curwood, James Oliver	$13.95	Softcover
1-4218-1120-0	The Circus Boys Across The Continent	Darlington, Edgar B.P.	$12.95	Softcover
1-4218-1121-9	The Circus Boys In Dixie Land	Darlington, Edgar B.P.	$12.95	Softcover
1-4218-1122-7	The Circus Boys on the Flying Rings	Darlington, Edgar B.P.	$12.95	Softcover
1-4218-1123-5	The Circus Boys On the Mississippi	Darlington, Edgar B.P.	$12.95	Softcover
1-59540-018-4	The Autobiography of Charles Darwin, Francis		$10.95	Softcover

ISBN	TITLE	AUTHOR	RETAIL	EDITION
	Darwin			
1-4218-0472-7	The Daredevil	Daviess, Maria Thompson	$12.95	Softcover
1-59540-604-2	Indian Games	Davis, Andrew McFarland	$10.95	Softcover
1-59540-640-9	Medieval Europe	Davis, H. W. C.	$11.95	Softcover
1-59540-115-6	Notes of a War Correspondent	Davis, R. H.	$11.95	Softcover
1-4218-1178-2	Captain Macklin	Davis, Richard Harding	$12.95	Softcover
1-59540-685-9	Cuba In War Time	Davis, Richard Harding	$10.95	Softcover
1-59540-686-7	Real Soldiers of Fortune	Davis, Richard Harding	$11.95	Softcover
1-59540-687-5	The Red Cross Girl	Davis, Richard Harding	$13.95	Softcover
1-59540-616-6	This Simian World	Day Jr., Clarence	$10.95	Softcover
1-4218-1548-6	An Old Maid	De Balzac, Honore	$11.95	Softcover
1-4218-1549-4	Massimilla Doni	De Balzac, Honore	$10.95	Softcover
1-4218-1550-8	The Marriage Contract	De Balzac, Honore	$11.95	Softcover
1-59540-040-0	Lost in the Fog	De Mille, James	$13.95	Softcover
1-59540-619-0	Robinson Crusoe	Defoe, Daniel	$15.95	Softcover
1-4218-0919-2	Robinson Crusoe	Defoe, Daniel	$31.95	Hardcover
1-59540-620-4	The Consolidator	Defoe, Daniel	$12.95	Softcover
1-59540-121-0	Two Years in the Forbidden City	Der Ling, The Princess	$14.95	Softcover
1-4218-0671-1	Two Years in the Forbidden City	Der Ling, The Princess	$29.95	Hardcover
1-59540-449-X	Discourse On The Method Of Rightly...	Descartes, Rene	$10.95	Softcover
1-59540-010-9	A Christmas Carol	Dickens, Charles	$10.95	Softcover
1-4218-0610-X	A Christmas Carol	Dickens, Charles	$26.95	Hardcover
1-59540-419-8	A Tale Of Two Cities	Dickens, Charles	$21.95	Softcover
1-4218-0819-6	A Tale Of Two Cities	Dickens, Charles	$39.95	Hardcover
1-59540-420-1	Great Expectations	Dickens, Charles	$26.95	Softcover
1-4218-0820-X	Great Expectations	Dickens, Charles	$45.95	Hardcover
1-4218-1517-6	Pictures from Italy	Dickens, Charles	$12.95	Softcover
1-59540-015-X	Poems, Series 1	Dickinson, Emily	$10.95	Softcover
1-59540-016-8	Poems, Series 2	Dickinson, Emily	$10.95	Softcover
1-4218-0616-9	Poems, Series 2	Dickinson, Emily	$26.95	Hardcover
1-59540-606-9	Four Girls and A Compact	Donnell, Annie Hamilton	$10.95	Softcover
1-59540-607-7	Rebecca Mary	Donnell, Annie	$10.95	Softcover

ISBN	TITLE	AUTHOR	RETAIL	EDITION
1-59540-023-0	Notes from the Underground	Hamilton Dostoyevsky, Fyodor	$11.95	Softcover
1-4218-0623-1	Notes from the Underground	Dostoyevsky, Fyodor	$26.95	Hardcover
1-4218-0128-0	The Gambler	Dostoyevsky, Fyodor	$12.95	Softcover
1-59540-400-7	A Study In Scarlet	Doyle, Arthur Conan	$11.95	Softcover
1-59540-401-5	Beyond The City	Doyle, Arthur Conan	$11.95	Softcover
1-59540-402-3	Memoirs Of Sherlock Holmes	Doyle, Arthur Conan	$14.95	Softcover
1-59540-403-1	Rodney Stone	Doyle, Arthur Conan	$14.95	Softcover
1-59540-404-X	Round The Red Lamp	Doyle, Arthur Conan	$13.95	Softcover
1-59540-206-3	Sir Nigel	Doyle, Arthur Conan	$18.95	Softcover
1-4218-0706-8	Sir Nigel	Doyle, Arthur Conan	$35.95	Hardcover
1-59540-405-8	Tales Of Terror And Mystery	Doyle, Arthur Conan	$13.95	Softcover
1-59540-406-6	The Adventures Of Gerard	Doyle, Arthur Conan	$12.95	Softcover
1-59540-407-4	The Adventures Of Sherlock Holmes	Doyle, Arthur Conan	$14.95	Softcover
1-59540-408-2	The Captain Of The Polestar	Doyle, Arthur Conan	$14.95	Softcover
1-59540-409-0	The Great Boer War	Doyle, Arthur Conan	$26.95	Softcover
1-59540-410-4	The Hound Of Baskervilles	Doyle, Arthur Conan	$12.95	Softcover
1-4218-0810-2	The Hound Of Baskervilles	Doyle, Arthur Conan	$27.95	Hardcover
1-59540-411-2	The Lost World	Doyle, Arthur Conan	$13.95	Softcover
1-4218-0811-0	The Lost World	Doyle, Arthur Conan	$28.95	Hardcover
1-59540-207-1	The New Revelation	Doyle, Arthur Conan	$10.95	Softcover
1-59540-412-0	The Poison Belt	Doyle, Arthur Conan	$10.95	Softcover
1-4218-0812-9	The Poison Belt	Doyle, Arthur Conan	$26.95	Hardcover
1-59540-413-9	The Return Of Sherlock Holmes	Doyle, Arthur Conan	$17.95	Softcover
1-59540-414-7	The Sign Of Four	Doyle, Arthur Conan	$11.95	Softcover
1-4218-0814-5	The Sign Of Four	Doyle, Arthur Conan	$26.95	Hardcover
1-59540-415-5	The Stark Munro Letters	Doyle, Arthur Conan	$13.95	Softcover
1-59540-416-3	The Valley Of Fear	Doyle, Arthur Conan	$12.95	Softcover
1-4218-0816-1	The Valley Of Fear	Doyle, Arthur Conan	$27.95	Hardcover
1-59540-417-1	The Vital Message	Doyle, Arthur Conan	$10.95	Softcover
1-59540-418-X	The White Company	Doyle, Arthur Conan	$21.95	Softcover
1-4218-1183-9	The Boy Allies Under the Sea	Drake, Robert L.	$12.95	Softcover
1-4218-1182-0	The Boy Allies with the Victorious Fleets	Drake, Robert L.	$12.95	Softcover
1-4218-1181-2	The Boy Allies with Uncle Sams Cruisers	Drake, Robert L.	$12.95	Softcover
1-4218-0484-0	The Boy Allies at Jutland	Drake, Robert L.	$13.95	Softcover

ISBN	TITLE	AUTHOR	RETAIL	EDITION
1-4218-0483-2	The Boy Allies Under Two Flags	Drake, Robert L.	$13.95	Softcover
1-59540-820-7	The Brighton Boys with the Flying Corps	Driscoll, James R.	$11.95	Softcover
1-59540-821-5	The Brighton Boys with the Submarine Fleet	Driscoll, James R.	$11.95	Softcover
1-59540-603-4	The Black Tulip	Dumas, Alexandre	$15.95	Softcover
1-59540-002-8	The Goodness of St.Rocque	Dunbar, Alice	$10.95	Softcover
1-4218-1532-X	The Boy Scout Aviators	Durston, George	$10.95	Softcover
1-4218-1533-8	The Boy Scouts in front of Warsaw	Durston, George	$10.95	Softcover
1-59540-009-5	Indian Heroes and Great Chieftains	Eastman, Charles A.	$10.95	Softcover
1-4218-0443-3	A Question	Ebers, Georg	$10.95	Softcover
1-4218-0471-9	Castle Rackrent	Edgeworth, Maria	$11.95	Softcover
1-59540-428-7	Silas Marner	Eliot, George	$13.95	Softcover
1-4218-0828-5	Silas Marner	Eliot, George	$28.95	Hardcover
1-59540-825-8	Thomas Jefferson	Ellis, Edward S.	$11.95	Softcover
1-4218-1526-5	Thomas Jefferson	Ellis, Edward S.	$11.95	Softcover
1-59540-445-7	Essays Series 1	Emerson, Ralph Waldo	$13.95	Softcover
1-4218-0845-5	Essays Series 1	Emerson, Ralph Waldo	$28.95	Hardcover
1-59540-446-5	Essays Series 2	Emerson, Ralph Waldo	$11.95	Softcover
1-4218-0846-3	Essays Series 2	Emerson, Ralph Waldo	$26.95	Hardcover
1-59540-447-3	Representative Men	Emerson, Ralph Waldo	$12.95	Softcover
1-4218-0847-1	Representative Men	Emerson, Ralph Waldo	$27.95	Hardcover
1-59540-448-1	The Conduct Of Life	Emerson, Ralph Waldo	$12.95	Softcover
1-4218-0848-X	The Conduct Of Life	Emerson, Ralph Waldo	$27.95	Hardcover
1-4218-0436-0	A Heroine of France	Everett-Green, Evelyn	$13.95	Softcover
1-4218-0457-3	The Mason-Bees	Fabre, J Henri	$12.95	Softcover
1-4218-1518-4	Laugh and Live	Fairbanks, Douglas	$10.95	Softcover
1-59540-025-7	A Simple Soul	Flaubert, Gustave	$10.95	Softcover
1-59540-026-5	Madame Bovary	Flaubert, Gustave	$18.95	Softcover
1-4218-0626-6	Madame Bovary	Flaubert, Gustave	$35.95	Hardcover
1-4218-1149-9	The Middle of Things	Fletcher, J.S.	$13.95	Softcover
1-4218-1150-2	The Orange-Yellow Diamond	Fletcher, J.S.	$13.95	Softcover
1-4218-0435-2	The Boy Life of Napoleon	Foa, Eugenie	$11.95	Softcover

ISBN	TITLE	AUTHOR	RETAIL	EDITION
1-59540-034-6	My Life and Work	Ford, Henry Jones	$14.95	Softcover
1-4218-0634-7	My Life and Work	Ford, Henry Jones	$29.95	Hardcover
1-59540-435-X	The Cleveland Era	Ford, Henry Jones	$11.95	Softcover
1-59540-691-3	A Young Girl's Diary	Freud, Sigmund	$13.95	Softcover
1-59540-306-X	The Wagner Story Book	Frost, Henry	$11.95	Softcover
1-59540-117-2	A Boy's Will	Frost, Robert	$10.95	Softcover
1-59540-118-0	North of Boston	Frost, Robert	$10.95	Softcover
1-4218-1180-4	October Vagabonds	Gallienne, Richard Le	$10.95	Softcover
1-4218-1561-3	Curly and Floppy Twistytail	Garis, Howard R.	$11.95	Softcover
1-4218-1562-1	Daddy takes us to the Garden	Garis, Howard R.	$10.95	Softcover
1-4218-1563-X	Dick Hamiltons Airship	Garis, Howard R.	$13.95	Softcover
1-4218-1564-8	Lulu, Alice and Jammie Wibble Wobble	Garis, Howard R.	$11.95	Softcover
1-4218-1565-6	Sammie and Susie Littletail	Garis, Howard R.	$11.95	Softcover
1-4218-1566-4	The Curlytops at Uncle Franks Ranch	Garis, Howard R.	$11.95	Softcover
1-4218-1567-2	The Curlytops on Star Island	Garis, Howard R.	$11.95	Softcover
1-59540-656-5	Umboo, The Elephant	Garis, Howard R.	$10.95	Softcover
1-4218-1568-0	Uncle Wiggily's Adventures	Garis, Howard R.	$11.95	Softcover
1-4218-1569-9	Uncle Wiggily's Travels	Garis, Howard R.	$11.95	Softcover
1-59540-621-2	Lady Into Fox	Garnett, David	$10.95	Softcover
1-4218-1130-8	My Lady Ludlow	Gaskell, Elizabeth	$12.95	Softcover
1-59540-627-1	Cousin Phillis	Gaskell, Elizabeth Cleghorn	$10.95	Softcover
1-4218-0927-3	Cousin Phillis	Gaskell, Elizabeth Cleghorn	$26.95	Hardcover
1-59540-681-6	Aunt Judy's Tales	Gatty, Mrs. Alfred	$11.95	Softcover
1-59540-665-4	The Beggar's Opera	Gay, John	$10.95	Softcover
1-59540-651-4	The Civilization of China	Giles, Herbert A.	$11.95	Softcover
1-4218-1146-4	Angel Island	Gillmore, Inez Haynes	$12.95	Softcover
1-4218-1118-9	Herland	Gilman, Charlotte Perkins Stetson	$12.95	Softcover
1-59540-666-2	The Burning Spear	Glasworthy, John	$12.95	Softcover
1-59540-046-X	The Wind in the Willows	Grahame, Kenneth	$12.95	Softcover
1-4218-0646-0	The Wind in the Willows	Grahame, Kenneth	$27.95	Hardcover
1-59540-124-5	The Personal Memoirs of U.S. Grant, Vol 1.	Grant, U. S.	$18.95	Softcover
1-4218-0674-6	The Personal Memoirs of U.S. Grant, Vol 1.	Grant, U. S.	$35.95	Hardcover
1-59540-125-3	The Personal Memoirs of U.S. Grant, Vol 2.	Grant, U. S.	$21.95	Softcover

ISBN	TITLE	AUTHOR	RETAIL	EDITION
1-4218-0675-4	The Personal Memoirs of U.S. Grant, Vol 2.	Grant, U. S.	$39.95	Hardcover
1-4218-1129-4	The Ways of Men	Gregory, Eliot	$13.95	Softcover
1-59540-532-1	Betty Zane	Grey, Zane	$15.95	Softcover
1-59540-533-X	Desert Gold	Grey, Zane	$17.95	Softcover
1-4218-0883-8	Desert Gold	Grey, Zane	$33.95	Hardcover
1-59540-534-8	Riders Of Purple Sage	Grey, Zane	$17.95	Softcover
1-59540-535-6	The Border Legion	Grey, Zane	$15.95	Softcover
1-4218-0885-4	The Border Legion	Grey, Zane	$31.95	Hardcover
1-59540-536-4	The Call Of The Canyon	Grey, Zane	$13.95	Softcover
1-4218-0886-2	The Call Of The Canyon	Grey, Zane	$28.95	Hardcover
1-59540-537-2	The Heritage Of The Desert	Grey, Zane	$14.95	Softcover
1-4218-0887-0	The Heritage Of The Desert	Grey, Zane	$29.95	Hardcover
1-59540-538-0	The Last Of The Plainsman	Grey, Zane	$13.95	Softcover
1-4218-0888-9	The Last Of The Plainsman	Grey, Zane	$28.95	Hardcover
1-59540-539-9	The Light Of The Western Stars	Grey, Zane	$18.95	Softcover
1-4218-0889-7	The Light Of The Western Stars	Grey, Zane	$35.95	Hardcover
1-59540-540-2	The Lone Star Ranger	Grey, Zane	$15.95	Softcover
1-4218-0890-0	The Lone Star Ranger	Grey, Zane	$31.95	Hardcover
1-59540-541-0	The Man Of The Forest	Grey, Zane	$20.95	Softcover
1-4218-0891-9	The Man Of The Forest	Grey, Zane	$37.95	Hardcover
1-59540-542-9	The Rainbow Trail	Grey, Zane	$15.95	Softcover
1-4218-0892-7	The Rainbow Trail	Grey, Zane	$31.95	Hardcover
1-59540-543-7	The Redheaded Outfield	Grey, Zane	$12.95	Softcover
1-59540-544-5	The Spirit Of The Border	Grey, Zane	$15.95	Softcover
1-4218-0894-3	The Spirit Of The Border	Grey, Zane	$31.95	Hardcover
1-59540-545-3	The U.P. Trail	Grey, Zane	$20.95	Softcover
1-4218-0895-1	The U.P. Trail	Grey, Zane	$37.95	Hardcover
1-59540-546-1	The Young Forester	Grey, Zane	$12.95	Softcover
1-4218-0896-X	The Young Forester	Grey, Zane	$27.95	Hardcover
1-59540-547-X	To The Last Man	Grey, Zane	$15.95	Softcover
1-4218-0897-8	To The Last Man	Grey, Zane	$31.95	Hardcover
1-59540-548-8	Wildfire	Grey, Zane	$17.95	Softcover
1-4218-0898-6	Wildfire	Grey, Zane	$33.95	Hardcover
1-4218-1581-8	The Inn at the Red Oak	Griswold, Latta	$12.95	Softcover
1-59540-667-0	Helen's Babies	Habberton, John	$11.95	Softcover

ISBN	TITLE	AUTHOR	RETAIL	EDITION
1-59540-639-5	Black Heart and White Heart	Haggard, H. Rider	$10.95	Softcover
1-4218-0450-6	The High School Boy's Training Hike	Hancock, H. Irving	$12.95	Softcover
1-59540-549-6	A Changed Man	Hardy, Thomas	$15.95	Softcover
1-59540-518-6	A Group Of Noble Dames	Hardy, Thomas	$13.95	Softcover
1-59540-519-4	A Pair Of Blue Eyes	Hardy, Thomas	$21.95	Softcover
1-4218-0869-2	A Pair Of Blue Eyes	Hardy, Thomas	$39.95	Hardcover
1-59540-520-8	Far From The Madding Crowd	Hardy, Thomas	$20.95	Softcover
1-59540-521-6	Lifes Little Ironies	Hardy, Thomas	$14.95	Softcover
1-59540-522-4	The Mayor Of Casterbridge	Hardy, Thomas	$17.95	Softcover
1-4218-0872-2	The Mayor Of Casterbridge	Hardy, Thomas	$33.95	Hardcover
1-59540-523-2	The Trumpet Major	Hardy, Thomas	$18.95	Softcover
1-59540-524-0	The Well Beloved	Hardy, Thomas	$13.95	Softcover
1-59540-525-9	Two On A Tower	Hardy, Thomas	$17.95	Softcover
1-59540-020-6	Oscar Wilde, His Life and Confessions, Volume 1	Harris, Frank	$13.95	Softcover
1-4218-0620-7	Oscar Wilde, His Life and Confessions, Volume 1	Harris, Frank	$28.95	Hardcover
1-59540-112-1	Biographical Stories	Hawthorne, Nathaniel	$10.95	Softcover
1-59540-113-X	The Great Stone Face	Hawthorne, Nathaniel	$10.95	Softcover
1-59540-683-2	The House of The Seven Gables	Hawthorne, Nathaniel	$15.95	Softcover
1-59540-671-9	The Lock and Key Library	Hawthrone, Julian	$13.95	Softcover
1-4218-0162-0	The Lock And Key Library Classic Mystrey and Detective Stories	Hawthrone, Julian	$18.95	Softcover
1-4218-1578-8	The Subterranean Brotherhood	Hawthrone, Julian	$13.95	Softcover
1-4218-0424-7	The Boy Allies at Verdun	Hayes, Clair W.	$13.95	Softcover
1-4218-1138-3	Jack Archer	Henty, G.A.	$14.95	Softcover
1-4218-1140-5	The Boy Knight	Henty, G.A.	$14.95	Softcover
1-4218-1156-1	Java Head	Hergesheimer, Joseph	$12.95	Softcover
1-4218-0452-2	Siddhartha	Hesse, Herman	$11.95	Softcover
1-4218-0352-6	Siddhartha	Hesse, Herman	$26.95	Hardcover
1-59540-021-4	On the Trail of Grant and Lee	Hill, Frederick Trevor	$12.95	Softcover
1-4218-0480-8	A Yankee in the Trenches	Holmes, R. Derby	$11.95	Softcover
1-59540-148-2	Iliad of Homer	Homer	$18.95	Softcover
1-4218-0698-3	Iliad of Homer	Homer	$35.95	Hardcover
1-4218-1165-0	Bunny Brown and his Sister Sue	Hope, Laura Lee	$11.95	Softcover

ISBN	TITLE	AUTHOR	RETAIL	EDITION
1-4218-1166-9	Six Little Bunkers at Grandma Bell's	Hope, Laura Lee	$11.95	Softcover
1-4218-1170-7	The Bobbsey Twins at the Seashore	Hope, Laura Lee	$11.95	Softcover
1-4218-1167-7	The Bobbsey Twins on A House Boat	Hope, Laura Lee	$12.95	Softcover
1-4218-1163-4	The Outdoor Girls at Rainbow Lake	Hope, Laura Lee	$11.95	Softcover
1-4218-1162-6	The Outdoor Girls at the Hostess House	Hope, Laura Lee	$11.95	Softcover
1-4218-1160-X	The Outdoor Girls at Wild Rose Lodge	Hope, Laura Lee	$11.95	Softcover
1-4218-1161-8	The Outdoor Girls in Army Service	Hope, Laura Lee	$11.95	Softcover
1-4218-1164-2	The Outdoor Girls of Deepdale	Hope, Laura Lee	$11.95	Softcover
1-59540-103-2	The Bobbsey Twins at Meadow Brook	Hope, Laura Lee	$12.95	Softcover
1-4218-0653-3	The Bobbsey Twins at Meadow Brook	Hope, Laura Lee	$27.95	Hardcover
1-59540-104-0	The Bobbsey Twins at School	Hope, Laura Lee	$11.95	Softcover
1-4218-0654-1	The Bobbsey Twins at School	Hope, Laura Lee	$26.95	Hardcover
1-59540-673-5	The Bobbsey Twins at Snow Lodge	Hope, Laura Lee	$11.95	Softcover
1-4218-1582-6	The Bobbsey Twins in a Great City	Hope, Laura Lee	$12.95	Softcover
1-59540-105-9	The Bobbsey Twins in the Country	Hope, Laura Lee	$12.95	Softcover
1-4218-0655-X	The Bobbsey Twins in the Country	Hope, Laura Lee	$27.95	Hardcover
1-4218-0465-4	The Bobbsey Twins in the Great West	Hope, Laura Lee	$12.95	Softcover
1-59540-674-3	The Bobbsey Twins in Washington	Hope, Laura Lee	$12.95	Softcover
1-59540-433-3	Miracle Mongers	Houdini, Harry	$11.95	Softcover
1-4218-0833-1	Miracle Mongers	Houdini, Harry	$26.95	Hardcover
1-4218-1132-4	The Covered Wagon	Hough, Emerson	$14.95	Softcover
1-4218-1131-6	The Law of the Land	Hough, Emerson	$13.95	Softcover
1-4218-0425-5	The Were-Wolf	Housman, Clemence	$10.95	Softcover
1-4218-0466-2	The Blue Moon	Housman, Laurence	$10.95	Softcover
1-4218-1196-0	Questionable Shapes	Howells, William Dean	$11.95	Softcover
1-59540-122-9	Evolution And Ethics	Huxley, Thomas H.	$15.95	Softcover
1-59540-644-1	An Enemy of the People	Ibsen, Henrik	$11.95	Softcover
1-4218-0944-3	An Enemy of the People	Ibsen, Henrik	$26.95	Hardcover
1-4218-1576-1	One of Life's Slaves	Idemil Lie, Jonas Lauritz	$11.95	Softcover

ISBN	TITLE	AUTHOR	RETAIL	EDITION
1-59540-613-1	Shakespeare's Bones	Ingleby, C. M.	$10.95	Softcover
1-59540-027-3	A Book of Remarkable Criminals	Irving, H. B.	$14.95	Softcover
1-59540-126-1	The Legend of Sleepy Hollow	Irving, Washington	$10.95	Softcover
1-4218-1137-5	A Man and His Money	Isham, Frederic Stewart	$13.95	Softcover
1-59540-421-X	Essays Before a Sonata	Ives, Charles	$10.95	Softcover
1-59540-632-8	Peggy Stewart: Navy Girl at Home	Jackson, Gabrielle E.	$12.95	Softcover
1-59540-643-3	Between Whiles	Jackson, Helent Hunt	$12.95	Softcover
1-59540-670-0	English Fairy Tales	Jacobs, Joseph	$13.95	Softcover
1-59540-664-6	Mogens and Other Stories	Jacobsen, Jens Peter	$10.95	Softcover
1-4218-0964-8	Mogens and Other Stories	Jacobsen, Jens Peter	$26.95	Hardcover
1-4218-0445-X	Quit Your Worrying	James, George Wharton	$12.95	Softcover
1-59540-645-X	In the Cage	James, Henry	$10.95	Softcover
1-59540-646-8	The Altar of The Dead	James, Henry	$10.95	Softcover
1-59540-647-6	The Chaperon	James, Henry	$10.95	Softcover
1-59540-648-4	The Europeans	James, Henry	$12.95	Softcover
1-4218-0948-6	The Europeans	James, Henry	$27.95	Hardcover
1-59540-649-2	The Pupil	James, Henry	$10.95	Softcover
1-59540-650-6	The Turn of the Screw	James, Henry	$11.95	Softcover
1-4218-0950-8	The Turn of the Screw	James, Henry	$26.95	Hardcover
1-4218-0428-X	A Trip Abroad	Janes, Don Carlos	$11.95	Softcover
1-4218-0196-5	In The Sargasso Sea	Janvier, Thomas A.	$13.95	Softcover
1-4218-1179-0	The Amateur Poacher	Jefferies, Richard	$11.95	Softcover
1-59540-688-3	The Open Air	Jefferies, Richard	$13.95	Softcover
1-4218-0161-2	Three Men on the Bummel	Jerome, Jerome K.	$13.95	Softcover
1-4218-0476-X	Murder in Any Degree	Johnson, Owen	$13.95	Softcover
1-4218-0432-8	The Young Captives	Jones, Erasmus W.	$12.95	Softcover
1-59540-437-6	Dubliners	Joyce, James	$13.95	Softcover
1-4218-0837-4	Dubliners	Joyce, James	$28.95	Hardcover
1-59540-690-5	The Go Ahead Boy and the Racing Motor-Boat	Kay, Ross	$12.95	Softcover
1-59540-682-4	Little Citizens	Kelly, Myra	$11.95	Softcover
1-59540-693-X	The Imitation of Christ	Kempis, Thomas A	$14.95	Softcover
1-4218-0993-1	The Imitation of Christ	Kempis, Thomas A	$29.95	Hardcover
1-59540-309-4	State Of The Union Addresses	Kennedy, John F.	$10.95	Softcover
1-59540-234-9	Mozart The Man And The	Kerst, Friedrich	$10.95	Softcover

ISBN	TITLE	AUTHOR	RETAIL	EDITION
	Artist			
1-59540-628-X	The Education of the Child	Key, Ellen	$10.95	Softcover
1-4218-1135-9	The Old Gray Homestead	Keyes, Frances Parkinson	$12.95	Softcover
1-59540-622-0	The Flying Saucers are Real	Keyhole, Donald	$13.95	Softcover
1-4218-0922-2	The Flying Saucers are Real	Keyhole, Donald	$28.95	Hardcover
1-59540-602-6	Tales of Two Countries	Kielland, Alexander	$11.95	Softcover
1-59540-623-9	The Life and Perambulations of a Mouse	Kilner, Dorothy	$10.95	Softcover
1-4218-1113-8	The Inner Shrine	King, Basil	$13.95	Softcover
1-59540-612-3	The Conquest of Fear	King, Basil	$12.95	Softcover
1-4218-0912-5	The Conquest of Fear	King, Basil	$27.95	Hardcover
1-4218-0446-8	Balcony Stories	King, Grace E.	$10.95	Softcover
1-59540-614-X	The Ancien Regime	Kingsley, Charles	$10.95	Softcover
1-59540-615-8	The Hermits	Kingsley, Charles	$14.95	Softcover
1-59540-516-X	Captains Courageous	Kipling, Rudyard	$12.95	Softcover
1-59540-517-8	The Jungle Book	Kipling, Rudyard	$12.95	Softcover
1-4218-0867-6	The Jungle Book	Kipling, Rudyard	$27.95	Hardcover
1-4218-1117-0	The Lion and the Mouse	Klein, Charles	$13.95	Softcover
1-59540-663-8	The Hunchback	Knowles, James Sheridan	$10.95	Softcover
1-59540-684-0	The Long Chance	Kyne, Peter B.	$15.95	Softcover
1-4218-0188-4	The Treasure	Lagerlof, Selma	$10.95	Softcover
1-4218-0103-5	The Brown Fairy Book	Lang, Andrew	$15.95	Softcover
1-4218-0106-X	The Crimson Fairy Book	Lang, Andrew	$15.95	Softcover
1-4218-0105-1	The Lilac Fairy Book	Lang, Andrew	$15.95	Softcover
1-4218-0104-3	The Pink Fairy Book	Lang, Andrew	$15.95	Softcover
1-59540-003-6	The Valet's Tragedy	Lang, Andrew	$14.95	Softcover
1-4218-0107-8	The Violet Fairy Book	Lang, Andrew	$17.95	Softcover
1-4218-0184-1	The Peace Negotiations	Lansing, Robert	$14.95	Softcover
1-59540-618-2	Aaron's Rod	Lawrence, D. H.	$20.95	Softcover
1-4218-1119-7	The Trespasser	Lawrence, D.H.	$13.95	Softcover
1-4218-1195-2	The Boy Aviators' Treasure Quest	Lawton, Wilbur	$12.95	Softcover
1-59540-816-9	The Boy Aviators in Africa	Lawton, Wilbur	$12.95	Softcover
1-4218-1612-1	The Czar's Spy	Le Queux, William	$14.95	Softcover
1-59540-024-9	The Phantom of the Opera	Leroux, Gaston	$15.95	Softcover
1-4218-0624-X	The Phantom of the Opera	Leroux, Gaston	$31.95	Hardcover
1-4218-1102-2	Love at Second Sight	Leverson, Ada	$12.95	Softcover

ISBN	TITLE	AUTHOR	RETAIL	EDITION
1-4218-1101-4	Love's Shadow	Leverson, Ada	$12.95	Softcover
1-4218-1100-6	Tenterhooks	Leverson, Ada	$12.95	Softcover
1-4218-1592-3	Mother Stories	Lindsay, Maud	$10.95	Softcover
1-4218-0147-7	The Story of Doctor Dolittle	Lofting, Hugh	$10.95	Softcover
1-4218-0148-5	The Voyages of Doctor Dolittle	Lofting, Hugh	$14.95	Softcover
1-4218-1151-0	Jerry of the Islands	London, Jack	$13.95	Softcover
1-4218-1570-2	A Daughter of the Snows	London, Jack	$15.95	Softcover
1-4218-0458-1	Before Adam	London, Jack	$10.95	Softcover
1-4218-0358-5	Before Adam	London, Jack	$26.95	Hardcover
1-59540-659-X	Moon Face	London, Jack	$11.95	Softcover
1-59540-039-7	The Call of the Wild	London, Jack	$10.95	Softcover
1-4218-0639-8	The Call of the Wild	London, Jack	$26.95	Hardcover
1-4218-1571-0	The People of the Abyss	London, Jack	$13.95	Softcover
1-4218-1572-9	White Fang	London, Jack	$13.95	Softcover
1-59540-307-8	Evangeline	Longfellow, Henry Wadsworth	$10.95	Softcover
1-59540-308-6	Hyperion	Longfellow, Henry Wadsworth	$14.95	Softcover
1-4218-0758-0	Hyperion	Longfellow, Henry Wadsworth	$29.95	Hardcover
1-59540-035-4	The Song of Hiawatha	Longfellow, Henry Wadsworth	$11.95	Softcover
1-4218-0635-5	The Song of Hiawatha	Longfellow, Henry Wadsworth	$26.95	Hardcover
1-4218-1184-7	The Pleasures of Ignorance	Lynd, Robert	$11.95	Softcover
1-59540-641-7	Heroes Every Child Should Know	Mabie, Hamilton Wright	$15.95	Softcover
1-4218-1528-1	Katrine,	Macartney Lane, Enilor	$12.95	Softcover
1-4218-1534-6	A Double Story	MacDonald, George	$10.95	Softcover
1-4218-0130-2	Salted With Fire	MacDonald, George	$13.95	Softcover
1-4218-0131-0	The Elect Lady	MacDonald, George	$13.95	Softcover
1-4218-0132-9	The Flight of the Shadow	MacDonald, George	$13.95	Softcover
1-4218-1174-X	The Prince	Machiavelli, Nicolo	$11.95	Softcover
1-4218-0149-3	Beside The Bonnie Brier Bush	Maclaren, Ian	$12.95	Softcover
1-4218-0111-6	The Jewel City	Macomber, Ben	$12.95	Softcover
1-4218-0112-4	How to Live a Holy Life	Macomber, C. E.	$11.95	Softcover
1-4218-0439-5	The Collectors	Mather, Frank Jewett	$10.95	Softcover
1-4218-0163-9	If I Were King	McCarthy, Justin Huntly	$12.95	Softcover

ISBN	TITLE	AUTHOR	RETAIL	EDITION
1-4218-1527-3	The American Child	McCracken, Elizabeth	$10.95	Softcover
1-4218-1579-6	The Sorrows of a Show Girl	McGaffey, Kenneth	$10.95	Softcover
1-4218-0138-8	The Man on the Box	McGrath, Harold	$14.95	Softcover
1-4218-0166-3	A Girl of the People	Meade, L. T.	$12.95	Softcover
1-4218-0167-1	A Sweet Girl Graduate	Meade, L. T.	$14.95	Softcover
1-4218-1535-4	The Adventures of Harry Richmond, Book 1	Meredith, George	$10.95	Softcover
1-4218-1536-2	The Adventures of Harry Richmond, Book 2	Meredith, George	$10.95	Softcover
1-4218-1537-0	The Adventures of Harry Richmond, Book 3	Meredith, George	$10.95	Softcover
1-4218-1538-9	The Adventures of Harry Richmond, Book 4	Meredith, George	$10.95	Softcover
1-4218-1539-7	The Adventures of Harry Richmond, Book 5	Meredith, George	$10.95	Softcover
1-4218-1540-0	The Adventures of Harry Richmond, Book 6	Meredith, George	$10.95	Softcover
1-4218-1541-9	The Adventures of Harry Richmond, Book 7	Meredith, George	$10.95	Softcover
1-4218-1542-7	The Adventures of Harry Richmond, Book 8	Meredith, George	$10.95	Softcover
1-4218-0139-6	From One Generation to Another	Merriman, Henry Seton	$13.95	Softcover
1-4218-0140-X	The Isle of Unrest	Merriman, Henry Seton	$14.95	Softcover
1-4218-0172-8	The Happy Adventures	Middleton, Lydia Miller	$13.95	Softcover
1-4218-0400-X	Ladies Must Live	Miller, Alice Duer	$11.95	Softcover
1-4218-0102-7	The Happiest Time of Their Lives	Miller, Alice Duer	$13.95	Softcover
1-59540-048-6	Paradise Lost	Milton, John	$14.95	Softcover
1-4218-0648-7	Paradise Lost	Milton, John	$29.95	Hardcover
1-59540-049-4	Paradise Regained	Milton, John	$10.95	Softcover
1-59540-109-1	Anne Of Avonlea	Montgomery, Lucy Maud	$15.95	Softcover
1-4218-0659-2	Anne Of Avonlea	Montgomery, Lucy Maud	$31.95	Hardcover
1-59540-110-5	Anne Of Green Gables	Montgomery, Lucy Maud	$17.95	Softcover
1-4218-0660-6	Anne Of Green Gables	Montgomery, Lucy Maud	$33.95	Hardcover
1-59540-123-7	Utopia	More, Thomas	$10.95	Softcover
1-4218-0673-8	Utopia	More, Thomas	$26.95	Hardcover
1-59540-617-4	Bar-20 Days	Mulford, Clarence E.	$13.95	Softcover
1-4218-0434-4	Out of the Ashes	Mumford, Ethel Watts	$12.95	Softcover
1-59540-638-7	Beasts and Super-Beasts	Munro, H. H.	$13.95	Softcover

ISBN	TITLE	AUTHOR	RETAIL	EDITION
1-59540-625-5	Beautiful Stories from Shakespeare	Nesbit, E.	$12.95	Softcover
1-4218-0925-7	Beautiful Stories from Shakespeare	Nesbit, E.	$27.95	Hardcover
1-59540-434-1	The Boys Life of Abraham Lincoln	Nicolay, Helen	$11.95	Softcover
1-59540-022-2	Beyond Good and Evil	Nietzsche, Friedrich	$12.95	Softcover
1-4218-0622-3	Beyond Good and Evil	Nietzsche, Friedrich	$27.95	Hardcover
1-4218-0122-1	The Best British Short Stories of 1922	O'Biren, Edward J.	$18.95	Softcover
1-4218-0125-6	The Old Northwest	Ogg, Federick Austin	$11.95	Softcover
1-4218-0189-2	The Coming of Cuculain	O'Grady, Standish	$10.95	Softcover
1-59540-045-1	The Book of Tea	Okakura, Kakuzo	$10.95	Softcover
1-4218-0101-9	The Gentleman	Ollivant, Alfred	$15.95	Softcover
1-4218-0114-0	An Amiable Charlatan	Oppenheim, E. Phillips	$13.95	Softcover
1-4218-0115-9	The Avenger	Oppenheim, E. Phillips	$15.95	Softcover
1-4218-0116-7	The Devil's Paw	Oppenheim, E. Phillips	$13.95	Softcover
1-4218-0117-5	The Evil Shepherd	Oppenheim, E. Phillips	$14.95	Softcover
1-4218-0118-3	The Great Impersonation	Oppenheim, E. Phillips	$14.95	Softcover
1-4218-0018-7	The Great Impersonation	Oppenheim, E. Phillips	$29.95	Hardcover
1-4218-0119-1	The Great Secret	Oppenheim, E. Phillips	$15.95	Softcover
1-4218-1519-2	The Illustrious Prince	Oppenheim, E. Phillips	$15.95	Softcover
1-4218-0120-5	The Kingdom of The Blind	Oppenheim, E. Phillips	$14.95	Softcover
1-4218-1520-6	The Malefactor	Oppenheim, E. Phillips	$15.95	Softcover
1-4218-0121-3	The Mischief-Maker	Oppenheim, E. Phillips	$17.95	Softcover
1-4218-1521-4	The Vanished Messenger	Oppenheim, E. Phillips	$15.95	Softcover
1-4218-1522-2	The Yellow Crayon	Oppenheim, E. Phillips	$15.95	Softcover
1-59540-014-1	The Zeppelin's Passenger	Oppenheim, E. Phillips	$14.95	Softcover
1-4218-0158-2	The Nine-Tenths	Oppenheim, James	$14.95	Softcover
1-4218-0110-8	The Old Man in the Corner	Orczy, Baroness	$13.95	Softcover
1-59540-611-5	The Scarlet Pimpernel	Orczy, Baroness	$15.95	Softcover
1-4218-0911-7	The Scarlet Pimpernel	Orczy, Baroness	$31.95	Hardcover
1-4218-0108-6	I Will Repay	Orczy, Baroness Emmuska	$13.95	Softcover
1-4218-0008-X	I Will Repay	Orczy, Baroness Emmuska	$28.95	Hardcover
1-4218-0109-4	The Elusive Pimpernel	Orczy, Baroness Emmuska	$15.95	Softcover
1-4218-0009-8	The Elusive Pimpernel	Orczy, Baroness Emmuska	$31.95	Hardcover
1-4218-0173-6	Famous Affinities of History, Vol 1	Orr, Lyndon	$10.95	Softcover

ISBN	TITLE	AUTHOR	RETAIL	EDITION
1-4218-0174-4	Famous Affinities of History, Vol 2	Orr, Lyndon	$10.95	Softcover
1-4218-0175-2	Famous Affinities of History, Vol 3	Orr, Lyndon	$10.95	Softcover
1-4218-0176-0	Famous Affinities of History, Vol 4	Orr, Lyndon	$10.95	Softcover
1-59540-429-5	Animal Farm	Orwell, George	$10.95	Softcover
1-4218-0829-3	Animal Farm	Orwell, George	$26.95	Hardcover
1-59540-430-9	Burmese Days	Orwell, George	$15.95	Softcover
1-4218-0830-7	Burmese Days	Orwell, George	$31.95	Hardcover
1-59540-431-7	Coming Up For Air	Orwell, George	$13.95	Softcover
1-4218-0831-5	Coming Up For Air	Orwell, George	$28.95	Hardcover
1-59540-432-5	Nineteen Eighty Four	Orwell, George	$15.95	Softcover
1-4218-0832-3	Nineteen Eighty Four	Orwell, George	$31.95	Hardcover
1-4218-0170-1	Love, The Fiddler	Osbourne, Lloyd	$11.95	Softcover
1-4218-0171-X	The Motormaniacs	Osbourne, Lloyd	$10.95	Softcover
1-4218-0126-4	Beasts, Men and Gods	Ossendowski, Ferdinand	$14.95	Softcover
1-4218-0026-8	Beasts, Men and Gods	Ossendowski, Ferdinand	$29.95	Hardcover
1-4218-0159-0	The Minute Boys of Mohawk Valley	Otis, James	$14.95	Softcover
1-4218-0179-5	Jack Winters' Gridiron Chums	Overton, Mark	$11.95	Softcover
1-4218-0151-5	The Young Woodsman	Oxley, J. Macdonald	$10.95	Softcover
1-59540-147-4	Japanese Fairy Tales	Ozaki, Yei Theodora	$13.95	Softcover
1-4218-0415-8	The Schoolbook of Forestry	Pack, Charles Lathrop	$10.95	Softcover
1-4218-0127-2	The White Moll	Packard, Frank L.	$14.95	Softcover
1-59540-120-2	The Upanishads	Parmananda, Swami	$10.95	Softcover
1-4218-1529-X	The Pony Rider Boys in New Mexico	Patchin, Frank G.	$13.95	Softcover
1-4218-1530-3	The Pony Rider Boys in the Ozarks	Patchin, Frank G.	$13.95	Softcover
1-4218-0437-9	The Pony Rider Boys in the Grand Canyon	Patchin, Frank Gee	$12.95	Softcover
1-4218-0438-7	The Pony Rider Boys with The Texas Rangers	Patchin, Frank Gee	$12.95	Softcover
1-4218-1588-5	The Motor Girls	Penrose, Margret	$12.95	Softcover
1-4218-1590-7	The Motor Girls on a Tour	Penrose, Margret	$12.95	Softcover
1-4218-1589-3	The Motor Girls on Cedar Lake	Penrose, Margret	$12.95	Softcover
1-4218-0469-7	The Japanese Twins	Perkins, Lucy Fitch	$10.95	Softcover
1-59540-444-9	Alcibiades I & II	Plato	$11.95	Softcover
1-59540-423-6	Humorous Tales	Poe, Edgar Allan	$13.95	Softcover

ISBN	TITLE	AUTHOR	RETAIL	EDITION
1-4218-0823-4	Humorous Tales	Poe, Edgar Allan	$28.95	Hardcover
1-59540-426-0	Old World Romances	Poe, Edgar Allan	$10.95	Softcover
1-4218-0826-9	Old World Romances	Poe, Edgar Allan	$26.95	Hardcover
1-59540-424-4	Tales Of Illusion	Poe, Edgar Allan	$10.95	Softcover
1-4218-0824-2	Tales Of Illusion	Poe, Edgar Allan	$26.95	Hardcover
1-59540-425-2	Tales Of Science	Poe, Edgar Allan	$12.95	Softcover
1-59540-427-9	The Narrative Of Arthur Gordon	Poe, Edgar Allan	$13.95	Softcover
1-59540-017-6	Men Of Iron	Pyle, Ernie Howard	$13.95	Softcover
1-4218-0617-7	Men Of Iron	Pyle, Ernie Howard	$28.95	Hardcover
1-59540-655-7	The Merry Adventures of Robin Hood	Pyle, Howard	$17.95	Softcover
1-4218-1197-9	The Four Faces	Queux, William le	$14.95	Softcover
1-59540-694-8	The Caesars	Quincey, Thomas De	$12.95	Softcover
1-4218-1199-5	Mystic Christianity	Ramacharaka, Yogi	$12.95	Softcover
1-59540-609-3	The Crisis in Russia	Ransome, Arthur	$10.95	Softcover
1-4218-1591-5	Love Stories	Rhinehart, Mary Roberts	$13.95	Softcover
1-59540-626-3	Taken Alive	Roe, E. P.	$17.95	Softcover
1-4218-0473-5	Captivity and Restoration	Rowlandson, Mary	$10.95	Softcover
1-4218-0470-0	The Island of Faith	Sangster, Margaret E.	$10.95	Softcover
1-4218-0499-9	The Black Dwarf	Scott, Walter	$12.95	Softcover
1-4218-0441-7	The Moon Metal	Serviss, Garrett P.	$10.95	Softcover
1-4218-0442-5	The Second Deluge	Serviss, Garrett P.	$15.95	Softcover
1-4218-0447-6	A Woman Tenderfoot	Seton-Thompson, Grace Gallatin	$10.95	Softcover
1-4218-0479-4	Marvels of Modern Science	Severing, Paul	$11.95	Softcover
1-59540-605-0	Black Beauty	Sewell, Anna	$12.95	Softcover
1-59540-235-7	A Treatise on Parents and Children	Shaw, George Bernard	$11.95	Softcover
1-4218-0735-1	A Treatise on Parents and Children	Shaw, George Bernard	$26.95	Hardcover
1-59540-236-5	An Unsocial Socialist	Shaw, George Bernard	$15.95	Softcover
1-59540-237-3	Androcles and The Lion	Shaw, George Bernard	$10.95	Softcover
1-59540-238-1	Arms and the Man	Shaw, George Bernard	$10.95	Softcover
1-4218-0738-6	Arms and the Man	Shaw, George Bernard	$26.95	Hardcover
1-59540-239-X	Caesar And Cleopatra	Shaw, George Bernard	$11.95	Softcover
1-4218-0739-4	Caesar And Cleopatra	Shaw, George	$26.95	Hardcover

ISBN	TITLE	AUTHOR	RETAIL	EDITION
1-59540-240-3	Candida	Shaw, George Bernard	$10.95	Softcover
1-4218-0740-8	Candida	Shaw, George Bernard	$26.95	Hardcover
1-59540-241-1	Captain Brassbound's Conversion	Shaw, George Bernard	$10.95	Softcover
1-4218-0741-6	Captain Brassbound's Conversion	Shaw, George Bernard	$26.95	Hardcover
1-59540-242-X	Fanny's First Play	Shaw, George Bernard	$10.95	Softcover
1-4218-0742-4	Fanny's First Play	Shaw, George Bernard	$26.95	Hardcover
1-59540-243-8	Heartbreak House	Shaw, George Bernard	$12.95	Softcover
1-4218-0743-2	Heartbreak House	Shaw, George Bernard	$27.95	Hardcover
1-59540-244-6	John Bull's Other Island	Shaw, George Bernard	$11.95	Softcover
1-4218-0744-0	John Bull's Other Island	Shaw, George Bernard	$26.95	Hardcover
1-59540-245-4	Major Barbara	Shaw, George Bernard	$11.95	Softcover
1-4218-0745-9	Major Barbara	Shaw, George Bernard	$26.95	Hardcover
1-59540-246-2	Man and Superman	Shaw, George Bernard	$13.95	Softcover
1-4218-0746-7	Man and Superman	Shaw, George Bernard	$28.95	Hardcover
1-59540-247-0	Misalliance	Shaw, George Bernard	$10.95	Softcover
1-4218-0747-5	Misalliance	Shaw, George Bernard	$26.95	Hardcover
1-59540-248-9	Mrs Warren's Profession	Shaw, George Bernard	$10.95	Softcover
1-4218-0748-3	Mrs Warren's Profession	Shaw, George Bernard	$26.95	Hardcover
1-59540-249-7	Pygmalion	Shaw, George Bernard	$11.95	Softcover
1-4218-0749-1	Pygmalion	Shaw, George Bernard	$26.95	Hardcover
1-59540-300-0	The Devil's Disciple	Shaw, George Bernard	$10.95	Softcover
1-4218-0750-5	The Devil's Disciple	Shaw, George Bernard	$26.95	Hardcover
1-59540-301-9	The Doctor's Dilemma	Shaw, George Bernard	$11.95	Softcover
1-4218-0751-3	The Doctor's Dilemma	Shaw, George Bernard	$26.95	Hardcover
1-59540-302-7	The Perfect Wagnerite	Shaw, George Bernard	$11.95	Softcover

ISBN	TITLE	AUTHOR	RETAIL	EDITION
1-4218-0752-1	The Perfect Wagnerite	Bernard Shaw, George	$26.95	Hardcover
1-59540-303-5	The Philanderer	Bernard Shaw, George	$10.95	Softcover
1-4218-0753-X	The Philanderer	Bernard Shaw, George	$26.95	Hardcover
1-59540-304-3	You Never Can Tell	Bernard Shaw, George	$11.95	Softcover
1-4218-0754-8	You Never Can Tell	Bernard Shaw, George	$26.95	Hardcover
1-59540-111-3	Frankenstein	Shelley, Mary Wollstonecraft	$13.95	Softcover
1-4218-0661-4	Frankenstein	Shelley, Mary Wollstonecraft	$28.95	Hardcover
1-4218-0448-4	Simon Bolivar	Sherwell, Guillermo A.	$12.95	Softcover
1-59540-668-9	The Fifth String	Sousa, John Philip	$10.95	Softcover
1-59540-500-3	A Familiar Study Of Men And Books	Stevenson, R. L.	$14.95	Softcover
1-59540-502-X	Across The Plains	Stevenson, R. L.	$12.95	Softcover
1-4218-0852-8	Across The Plains	Stevenson, R. L.	$27.95	Hardcover
1-59540-501-1	An InLand Voyage	Stevenson, R. L.	$10.95	Softcover
1-4218-0851-X	An InLand Voyage	Stevenson, R. L.	$26.95	Hardcover
1-59540-503-8	Catriona	Stevenson, R. L.	$15.95	Softcover
1-4218-0853-6	Catriona	Stevenson, R. L.	$31.95	Hardcover
1-59540-504-6	In The South Seas	Stevenson, R. L.	$15.95	Softcover
1-4218-0854-4	In The South Seas	Stevenson, R. L.	$31.95	Hardcover
1-59540-505-4	Kidnapped	Stevenson, R. L.	$14.95	Softcover
1-4218-0855-2	Kidnapped	Stevenson, R. L.	$29.95	Hardcover
1-59540-506-2	Lay Morals	Stevenson, R. L.	$14.95	Softcover
1-59540-508-9	Memoir Of Fleeming Jenkin	Stevenson, R. L.	$11.95	Softcover
1-4218-0858-7	Memoir Of Fleeming Jenkin	Stevenson, R. L.	$26.95	Hardcover
1-59540-507-0	Memories And Portraits	Stevenson, R. L.	$11.95	Softcover
1-4218-0857-9	Memories And Portraits	Stevenson, R. L.	$26.95	Hardcover
1-59540-509-7	New Arabian Nights	Stevenson, R. L.	$15.95	Softcover
1-4218-0859-5	New Arabian Nights	Stevenson, R. L.	$31.95	Hardcover
1-59540-510-0	Records Of A Family Of Engineers	Stevenson, R. L.	$12.95	Softcover
1-59540-511-9	The Black Arrow	Stevenson, R. L.	$14.95	Softcover
1-59540-512-7	The Dynamiter	Stevenson, R. L.	$13.95	Softcover
1-4218-0862-5	The Dynamiter	Stevenson, R. L.	$28.95	Hardcover
1-59540-513-5	The Ebb Tide	Stevenson, R. L.	$11.95	Softcover

ISBN	TITLE	AUTHOR	RETAIL	EDITION
1-4218-0863-3	The Ebb Tide	Stevenson, R. L.	$26.95	Hardcover
1-59540-514-3	The Merry Men	Stevenson, R. L.	$14.95	Softcover
1-4218-0864-1	The Merry Men	Stevenson, R. L.	$29.95	Hardcover
1-59540-116-4	The Strange Case of Dr.Jekyll and Mr Hyde	Stevenson, R. L.	$10.95	Softcover
1-59540-515-1	Treasure Island	Stevenson, R. L.	$13.95	Softcover
1-4218-0865-X	Treasure Island	Stevenson, R. L.	$28.95	Hardcover
1-59540-007-9	The Jewel of Seven Stars	Stoker, Bram	$14.95	Softcover
1-4218-0607-X	The Jewel of Seven Stars	Stoker, Bram	$29.95	Hardcover
1-4218-1159-6	The Motor Maids in Fair Japan	Stokes, Katherine	$12.95	Softcover
1-59540-031-1	Uncle Tom's Cabin	Stowe, Harriet Beecher	$26.95	Softcover
1-4218-0631-2	Uncle Tom's Cabin	Stowe, Harriet Beecher	$45.95	Hardcover
1-4218-0493-X	The Path of Life	Streuvels, Stijn	$11.95	Softcover
1-59540-441-4	Gulliver's Travels	Swift, Jonathan	$15.95	Softcover
1-4218-0481-6	The Hungry Stones	Tagore, Rabindranath	$12.95	Softcover
1-4218-1115-4	Alice Adams	Tarkington, Booth	$14.95	Softcover
1-4218-0407-7	Beasley's Christmas Party	Tarkington, Booth	$10.95	Softcover
1-4218-0408-5	His Own People	Tarkington, Booth	$10.95	Softcover
1-4218-0406-9	The Beautiful Lady	Tarkington, Booth	$10.95	Softcover
1-59540-006-0	Beauty and The Beast	Taylor, Bayard	$14.95	Softcover
1-4218-0606-1	Beauty and The Beast	Taylor, Bayard	$29.95	Hardcover
1-4218-0440-9	The Principles of Scientific Management	Taylor, Frederick Winslow	$10.95	Softcover
1-4218-1198-7	Catherine: A Story	Thackeray, William Makepeace	$12.95	Softcover
1-59540-127-X	The Book of Snobs	Thackeray, William Makepeace	$13.95	Softcover
1-4218-0677-0	The Book of Snobs	Thackeray, William Makepeace	$28.95	Hardcover
1-59540-032-X	Walden	Thoreau, Henry David	$15.95	Softcover
1-4218-0632-0	Walden	Thoreau, Henry David	$31.95	Hardcover
1-59540-033-8	Walking	Thoreau, Henry David	$10.95	Softcover
1-4218-0477-8	The Sheridan Road Mystery	Thorne, Paul and Mabel	$12.95	Softcover
1-4218-1158-8	The Masquerader	Thurston, Katherine Cecil	$15.95	Softcover
1-4218-0467-0	Master and Man	Tolstoy, Leo	$10.95	Softcover
1-59540-675-1	The Cossacks	Tolstoy, Leo	$13.95	Softcover
1-4218-0975-3	The Cossacks	Tolstoy, Leo	$28.95	Hardcover

ISBN	TITLE	AUTHOR	RETAIL	EDITION
1-4218-0478-6	Bob Cook and the German Spy	Tomlinson, Paul G.	$12.95	Softcover
1-4218-0468-9	The Postmaster's Daughter	Tracy, Louis	$14.95	Softcover
1-4218-0413-1	In The Forest	Traill, Catherine Parr	$11.95	Softcover
1-4218-0444-1	A Voyage to the Moon	Tucker, George	$13.95	Softcover
1-4218-1148-0	The Jew and other stories	Turgenev, Ivan	$13.95	Softcover
1-4218-0433-6	Seven Little Australians	Turner, Ethel	$12.95	Softcover
1-59540-310-8	A Connecticut Yankee In King Arthur's Court	Twain, Mark	$17.95	Softcover
1-59540-311-6	A Horse's Tale	Twain, Mark	$10.95	Softcover
1-59540-312-4	Alonzo Fitz And Other Stories	Twain, Mark	$10.95	Softcover
1-59540-313-2	Christian Science	Twain, Mark	$13.95	Softcover
1-59540-314-0	Life On The Mississippi	Twain, Mark	$21.95	Softcover
1-59540-315-9	Roughing It	Twain, Mark	$22.95	Softcover
1-4218-0765-3	Roughing It	Twain, Mark	$41.95	Hardcover
1-59540-316-7	Sketches New And Old	Twain, Mark	$17.95	Softcover
1-4218-0766-1	Sketches New And Old	Twain, Mark	$33.95	Hardcover
1-59540-317-5	The Adventures Of Huckleberry Finn	Twain, Mark	$15.95	Softcover
1-4218-0767-X	The Adventures Of Huckleberry Finn	Twain, Mark	$31.95	Hardcover
1-59540-318-3	The Adventures Of Tom Sawyer	Twain, Mark	$13.95	Softcover
1-4218-0768-8	The Adventures Of Tom Sawyer	Twain, Mark	$28.95	Hardcover
1-59540-319-1	The American Claimant	Twain, Mark	$12.95	Softcover
1-59540-320-5	The Letters Of Mark Twain Vol.1	Twain, Mark	$11.95	Softcover
1-59540-321-3	The Letters Of Mark Twain Vol.2	Twain, Mark	$12.95	Softcover
1-59540-322-1	The Letters Of Mark Twain Vol.3	Twain, Mark	$13.95	Softcover
1-59540-323-X	The Letters Of Mark Twain Vol.4	Twain, Mark	$14.95	Softcover
1-59540-324-8	The Letters Of Mark Twain Vol.5 & 6	Twain, Mark	$12.95	Softcover
1-59540-325-6	The Man That Corrupted Hadleyburg	Twain, Mark	$18.95	Softcover
1-4218-0775-0	The Man That Corrupted Hadleyburg	Twain, Mark	$35.95	Hardcover
1-59540-326-4	The Mysterious Stranger	Twain, Mark	$11.95	Softcover
1-4218-0776-9	The Mysterious Stranger	Twain, Mark	$26.95	Hardcover
1-59540-327-2	The Prince And The Pauper	Twain, Mark	$14.95	Softcover
1-4218-0777-7	The Prince And The Pauper	Twain, Mark	$29.95	Hardcover

ISBN	TITLE	AUTHOR	RETAIL	EDITION
1-59540-328-0	The Tragedy of Pudd'nhead Wilson	Twain, Mark	$12.95	Softcover
1-59540-329-9	Tom Sawyer Abroad	Twain, Mark	$10.95	Softcover
1-59540-330-2	Tom Sawyer Detective	Twain, Mark	$10.95	Softcover
1-59540-331-0	What Is Man	Twain, Mark	$15.95	Softcover
1-4218-0781-5	What Is Man	Twain, Mark	$31.95	Hardcover
1-4218-1125-1	Aunt Jane's Nieces	Van Dyne, Edith	$12.95	Softcover
1-4218-1124-3	Aunt Jane's Nieces and Uncle John	Van Dyne, Edith	$11.95	Softcover
1-4218-1126-X	Aunt Jane's Nieces at Millville	Van Dyne, Edith	$12.95	Softcover
1-4218-1127-8	Aunt Jane's Nieces on Vacation	Van Dyne, Edith	$12.95	Softcover
1-4218-1523-0	Aunt Jane's Nieces at Work	Van Dyne, Edith	$12.95	Softcover
1-4218-1524-9	Aunt Jane's Nieces in Society	Van Dyne, Edith	$13.95	Softcover
1-4218-1525-7	Aunt Jane's Nieces out West	Van Dyne, Edith	$12.95	Softcover
1-59540-677-8	The Camp Fire Girls at Sunrise Hill	Vandercook, Margaret	$11.95	Softcover
1-59540-527-5	Stories By English Authors In Africa	Various Authors	$11.95	Softcover
1-59540-528-3	Stories By English Authors In France	Various Authors	$11.95	Softcover
1-59540-529-1	Stories By English Authors In Germany	Various Authors	$11.95	Softcover
1-59540-526-7	The Martin Luther King Jr	Various Authors	$18.95	Softcover
1-59540-042-7	Around the World in 80 Days	Verne, Jules	$13.95	Softcover
1-4218-0642-8	Around the World in 80 Days	Verne, Jules	$28.95	Hardcover
1-59540-043-5	From the Earth to the Moon and Round the Moon	Verne, Jules	$17.95	Softcover
1-4218-0643-6	From the Earth to the Moon and Round the Moon	Verne, Jules	$33.95	Hardcover
1-59540-044-3	Twenty Thousand Leagues Under The Sea	Verne, Jules	$17.95	Softcover
1-4218-0644-4	Twenty Thousand Leagues Under The Sea	Verne, Jules	$33.95	Hardcover
1-4218-0124-8	The Solitary Summer	Von Arnim, Elizabeth	$10.95	Softcover
1-4218-0024-1	The Solitary Summer	Von Arnim, Elizabeth	$26.95	Hardcover
1-4218-0454-9	The Castle of Otranto	Walpole, Horace	$10.95	Softcover
1-59540-657-3	The Cathedral	Walpole, Hugh	$21.95	Softcover
1-59540-699-9	The Pastor's Son	Walter, William W.	$10.95	Softcover
1-4218-0475-1	A Peep Behind the Scenes	Walton, O. F.	$13.95	Softcover
1-59540-001-X	Chaucer	Ward, Adolphus William	$12.95	Softcover
1-4218-0601-0	Chaucer	Ward, Adolphus	$27.95	Hardcover

ISBN	TITLE	AUTHOR	RETAIL	EDITION
1-4218-0456-5	A Great Success	William Ward, Humphry	$10.95	Softcover
1-4218-0414-X	Being A Boy	Warner, Charles Dudley	$10.95	Softcover
1-4218-1136-7	Jack of the Pony Express	Webster, Frank V.	$11.95	Softcover
1-4218-0409-3	Patty's Butterfly Days	Wells, Carolyn	$13.95	Softcover
1-4218-0412-3	Patty's Suitors	Wells, Carolyn	$14.95	Softcover
1-4218-0410-7	Raspberry Jam	Wells, Carolyn	$13.95	Softcover
1-4218-0411-5	The Gold Bag	Wells, Carolyn	$13.95	Softcover
1-59540-636-0	The First Men In The Moon	Wells, H. G.	$13.95	Softcover
1-4218-0936-2	The First Men In The Moon	Wells, H. G.	$28.95	Hardcover
1-59540-028-1	The Island of Doctor Moreau	Wells, H. G.	$11.95	Softcover
1-4218-0628-2	The Island of Doctor Moreau	Wells, H. G.	$26.95	Hardcover
1-59540-029-X	The Time Machine	Wells, H. G.	$10.95	Softcover
1-4218-0629-0	The Time Machine	Wells, H. G.	$26.95	Hardcover
1-59540-030-3	The War of the Worlds	Wells, H. G.	$12.95	Softcover
1-4218-0630-4	The War of the Worlds	Wells, H. G.	$27.95	Hardcover
1-59540-637-9	When The Sleeper Wakes	Wells, H. G.	$14.95	Softcover
1-4218-0937-0	When The Sleeper Wakes	Wells, H. G.	$29.95	Hardcover
1-4218-0489-1	Under the Red Robe	Weyman, Stanley	$13.95	Softcover
1-4218-0429-8	Bunner Sisters	Wharton, Edith	$10.95	Softcover
1-4218-0430-1	Tales of Men and Ghosts	Wharton, Edith	$15.95	Softcover
1-59540-012-5	A Book of Scoundrels	Whibley, Charles	$12.95	Softcover
1-4218-0492-1	Arizona Nights	White, Stewart Edward	$13.95	Softcover
1-4218-0490-5	The Call of the North	White, Stewart Edward	$11.95	Softcover
1-4218-0491-3	The Mountains	White, Stewart Edward	$12.95	Softcover
1-59540-332-9	An Ideal Husband	Wilde, Oscar	$11.95	Softcover
1-4218-0782-3	An Ideal Husband	Wilde, Oscar	$26.95	Hardcover
1-59540-333-7	Essays and Lectures	Wilde, Oscar	$11.95	Softcover
1-4218-0783-1	Essays and Lectures	Wilde, Oscar	$26.95	Hardcover
1-59540-334-5	Intentions	Wilde, Oscar	$12.95	Softcover
1-4218-0784-X	Intentions	Wilde, Oscar	$27.95	Hardcover
1-59540-335-3	Lord Arthur Savile's Crime	Wilde, Oscar	$11.95	Softcover
1-4218-0785-8	Lord Arthur Savile's Crime	Wilde, Oscar	$26.95	Hardcover
1-59540-336-1	Poems	Wilde, Oscar	$13.95	Softcover
1-4218-0786-6	Poems	Wilde, Oscar	$28.95	Hardcover
1-59540-337-X	Selected Prose of Oscar	Wilde, Oscar	$11.95	Softcover

ISBN	TITLE	AUTHOR	RETAIL	EDITION
1-4218-0787-4	Selected Prose of Oscar Wilde	Wilde, Oscar	$26.95	Hardcover
1-59540-114-8	The Importance of being Earnest	Wilde, Oscar	$10.95	Softcover
1-4218-0664-9	The Importance of being Earnest	Wilde, Oscar	$26.95	Hardcover
1-59540-338-8	The Picture Of Dorian Gray	Wilde, Oscar	$12.95	Softcover
1-4218-0788-2	The Picture Of Dorian Gray	Wilde, Oscar	$27.95	Hardcover
1-4218-0426-3	The Head Hunters of Northern Luzon	Willcox, Cornelis DeWitt	$12.95	Softcover
1-4218-0497-2	The Yellow Streak	Williams, Valentine	$14.95	Softcover
1-4218-0113-2	The Ghost of Guir House	Willing, Charles	$11.95	Softcover
1-4218-1109-X	The Rover Boys In The Mountains	Winfield, Arthur M.	$12.95	Softcover
1-59540-339-6	A Damsel In Distress	Wodehouse, P. G.	$14.95	Softcover
1-59540-340-X	Indiscretions of Archie	Wodehouse, P. G.	$15.95	Softcover
1-4218-0790-4	Indiscretions of Archie	Wodehouse, P. G.	$31.95	Hardcover
1-59540-341-8	Love Among The Chickens	Wodehouse, P. G.	$12.95	Softcover
1-4218-0791-2	Love Among The Chickens	Wodehouse, P. G.	$27.95	Hardcover
1-59540-342-6	The Clicking Of Cuthbert	Wodehouse, P. G.	$13.95	Softcover
1-4218-0792-0	The Clicking Of Cuthbert	Wodehouse, P. G.	$28.95	Hardcover
1-59540-343-4	The Coming Of Bill	Wodehouse, P. G.	$15.95	Softcover
1-4218-0793-9	The Coming Of Bill	Wodehouse, P. G.	$31.95	Hardcover
1-59540-344-2	The Gold Bat	Wodehouse, P. G.	$12.95	Softcover
1-4218-0794-7	The Gold Bat	Wodehouse, P. G.	$27.95	Hardcover
1-59540-345-0	The Head Of Kay's	Wodehouse, P. G.	$11.95	Softcover
1-4218-0795-5	The Head Of Kay's	Wodehouse, P. G.	$26.95	Hardcover
1-59540-346-9	The Intrusion Of Jimmy	Wodehouse, P. G.	$14.95	Softcover
1-4218-0796-3	The Intrusion Of Jimmy	Wodehouse, P. G.	$29.95	Hardcover
1-59540-347-7	The Little Nugget	Wodehouse, P. G.	$14.95	Softcover
1-4218-0797-1	The Little Nugget	Wodehouse, P. G.	$29.95	Hardcover
1-59540-348-5	The Little Warrior	Wodehouse, P. G.	$20.95	Softcover
1-59540-629-8	Back Home	Wood, Eugene	$12.95	Softcover
1-4218-0498-0	Jacob's Room	Woolf, Virginia	$12.95	Softcover
1-59540-349-3	Monday or Tuesday	Woolf, Virginia	$10.95	Softcover
1-59540-530-5	Night And Day	Woolf, Virginia	$22.95	Softcover
1-59540-531-3	The Voyage Out	Woolf, Virginia	$20.95	Softcover
1-59540-013-3	Abbeychurch	Yonge, Charlotte M	$14.95	Softcover

ISBN	TITLE	AUTHOR	RETAIL	EDITION
1-4218-0421-2	Countess Kate	Yonge, Charlotte M.	$12.95	Softcover
1-4218-0422-0	Friarswood Post-Office	Yonge, Charlotte M.	$13.95	Softcover
1-4218-0423-9	Grisly Grisell	Yonge, Charlotte M.	$13.95	Softcover
1-4218-0417-4	Pigeon Pie	Yonge, Charlotte M.	$10.95	Softcover
1-4218-0420-4	The Lances of Lynwood	Yonge, Charlotte M.	$12.95	Softcover
1-4218-0418-2	The Little Duke	Yonge, Charlotte M.	$11.95	Softcover
1-4218-0419-0	The Stokesley Secret	Yonge, Charlotte M.	$13.95	Softcover
1-4218-0449-2	A Boy's Ride	Zollinger, Gulielma	$13.95	Softcover

www.ingramcontent.com/pod-product-compliance
Lightning Source LLC
Chambersburg PA
CBHW031416040426
42444CB00005B/592